THIS
LOVE
IS FOR
YOU

KIMBERLY CARLTON

ISBN: 978-0-6927-1807-0

♥

DEDICATION

For the Divine spark that lights up all creation…
In all of Your forms as all of us

CONTENTS

♥

FOREWORD

I recently celebrated my 70th birthday. I certainly know that this does not automatically bring with it wisdom and discernment—in fact, I personally know any number of 70 year-old adolescents. But if I couple living that long with (1.) being a parent and grandparent, (2.) 35+ years of teaching and school administration experience, and (3.) 25+ years of private practice psychotherapy as a Marriage and Family Therapist, I think I have a proper perspective from which to judge the merits of this book.

I can point to a number of books that have been seminal in my own life. I keep a journal of favorite quotes that I treasure and look over regularly. Kimberly Carlton's book has provided me with many "pearls of wisdom" that have made their way into that reading journal. An avid reader myself, I have often recommended books to my students and my counseling clients. *This Love Is for You* is one of the books I will encourage others to read (and with pencil in-hand!). It encapsulates many of the "life lessons" that I have worked to impart to those in my care.

Kimberly fearlessly shares personal anecdotes to illustrate her journey; it takes real courage to be that transparent. While her life experience may be different from mine (and yours), the guiding principles are the same for all of us. Be kind—it is "the key to the doorway of love". Life is not so much "either/or" as much as "both/and". Forgiveness is essential. There is a gift hidden in every situation, even seemingly horrible ones. Be open to (in fact, pray for) that "spiritual bolt out of the blue" that can completely redirect our attention. Maybe this book will be such a "bolt" for you.

Kimberly's definition of love is a worldview that connects us to all creation. This is counter-cultural in a society that fosters narcissism. Her focus on love as action flies in the face of the contemporary emphasis on "how I feel." She further challenges us to assume personal responsibility for creating our own experience. "The quality of our thoughts determines the quality of our lives." She calls us to be positive, hopeful, and perhaps even a bit of a Pollyanna. She states that if we can change our thoughts, we can change our lives. Cognitive therapists have been telling us this for years, but Kimberly has a way of issuing this challenge in a way that is understandable and credible.

Some of her ponderings are simple and direct—you may have heard them a hundred times before but you will be grateful to hear them repeated. Others are creative and totally unique: e.g., thoughts are a marinade for the mind, and selective attention is comparable to aligning the tires on your car. Bottom line, Kimberly gets us to THINK. She wants us to CHOOSE. She wants us to know that we MATTER— that we have supreme VALUE. That is the message of this wise little book. You are special. You are loved. And this love is for you!

Gloria Ryan, LMFT

PREFACE

You've lived your entire life in accordance with a set of beliefs about the world and your place in it. We all have. What you believe is true about you affects your whole life.

I used to believe I was worthless and undeserving of love. I thought I had to meet expectations set by other people to even have a chance at being accepted by others. Somehow, though, whenever I thought I had reached the finish line in that race to measure up, it seemed the line was pushed farther out as soon as I approached it. Never feeling good enough, just not quite up to snuff, is one of the most painful and debilitating experiences I ever had. It hurts, deeply.

Now that I no longer feel that way, it's very clear to me that many people struggle and even suffer as much or more than I ever did from the same problem. I've spent the better part of three decades learning how to escape those painful feelings. I've learned some things along the way that have helped me tremendously. Maybe sharing them could help others, too. That's the reason for this book. If something in here helps someone reading this, then my experience will have served a useful purpose beyond teaching just me how to live a more joyful and peaceful life.

The only things we lack are those we withhold from ourselves. In my case, it was definitely not obvious to me at the time that I was denying myself the experience of love in response to my feelings of unworthiness. Yet, when the insight came that this is precisely why I felt love to be lacking in my life, my willingness to look beneath the surface and challenge my own assumptions is what allowed that life-changing insight to enter my awareness. Thus began a lifelong journey of spiritual exploration that has brought me out from the deepest darkness into a life of light and love.

I won't lie and say the journey has been an easy one, but I can say unequivocally that it has been worthwhile. In fact, I wouldn't trade it for anything. Life can feel like a living hell or it can feel like heaven on Earth and, having been in both places, I can tell you that moving from one to the other can be a lot more straightforward than you might think. You have a lot more control over which you reside in than you might realize. And you have a lot more to gain from learning what makes the difference between these two options than you might be able to imagine right now.

Opening our hearts and minds can seem risky, perhaps even terrifyingly dangerous. Fear is always a block to love. However, we must face fear because life is not for the faint of heart. Calling on our courage strengthens us, so I encourage you to delve fearlessly into exploring your most fundamental beliefs. You may discover, as I did, that the love you give to yourself and others frees you from fear and opens you up to receive the richest blessings life has to offer.

♥

ACKNOWLEDGEMENTS

"I have sent you nothing but angels."[1]

I am unspeakably grateful to all the angels who have crossed my path and blessed my life. No list can be complete but mine must include the following individuals: Oleg Lobykin, Nika Lobykina, Kari Carlton, Terri & Doug McGinnis, Gary & Wendy Carlton, Mark McMaster, Denis & Gloria Ryan, Omer & Shirley Nadeau, Nancy Glaser, and Steve Caron.

In addition, I have been inspired and learned so much from many spiritual teachers, whose gifts I could never repay: Neale Donald Walsch, Dr. Wayne W. Dyer, Marianne Williamson, Eckhart Tolle, Deepak Chopra, Dr. David R. Hawkins, Paulo Coelho, Trevor Blake, Don Miguel Ruiz, Esther & Jerry Hicks and Abraham, among many others.

I thank the Alpha and Omega, and all in between.

---

[1] Neale Donald Walsch, *Conversations With God, Book 2* (Charlottesville, VA: Hampton Roads, 1997), p. 177.

♥

WHAT IS LOVE?

I grew up with the persistent sense that love was scarce. I know I never felt like I had enough of it, and this was clearest when I felt lonely and misunderstood.

Later I began to notice that people would often claim to love me despite behaving in ways that I found hurtful. In fact, love was even used as an excuse for selfish or insensitive actions, as if love was a magic word that made everything OK even when I could clearly see that it was anything but OK.

I began to hear love defined and described not as a feeling, but instead as a behavior. "Love is a verb" seemed to go a long way toward solving the problem of the discrepancy between people's proclamations and their behaviors. If love was a verb, then it's identifiable by the actions we can observe. No one can try to convince me they love me if what they do is inconsistent with the word.

Yet somehow this definition, although perhaps

better than the first, also failed to satisfy me. For one thing, it seemed to separate actions from their intentions, so at best it felt incomplete. I'd heard "the road to hell is paved with good intentions" and that seemed to point to an essential truth: intentions are not actions, and they can be misconstrued or even abused as excuses. What difference does it really make when someone claims after doing something that hurts us that they didn't mean to cause harm? Yet the reverse must also be true: if beneficial actions do not come from good intent, how praiseworthy can they be?

Somewhere along the way I heard about this idea called unconditional love. This really grabbed my attention because I'd so often felt that I had to do or be what someone else wanted to "earn" their love, and that was always a painful exercise in futility. Nothing was ever good enough, and I never felt good enough. So unconditional love felt much more true to me as an idea of what love is.

I believed in God from a very early age, as far back as I can remember. I was baptized a Catholic as a baby, and then almost 18 years later I chose to be baptized a Mormon. Very shortly thereafter, I left all organized religion behind because none that I tried felt in alignment with what I knew of God. To me, God was always love.

Unconditional love was the only way I knew or could understand God. Of course, if unconditional love is closest to my ideal of love, then conditional love must not really be love at all. That means the term "unconditional love" is redundant because the adjective "unconditional" is really an attribute intrinsic to love.

By now I was starting to better understand what this word "love" means, but still it seemed mysterious. On top of that, a friend in college I loved once observed to me that the word has been used by so many people in so many different ways as to render it essentially meaningless.

I found this observation to be both true and deeply offensive. Love has always been a central concern in my life, and it's a real problem if the word is meaningless.

I've come to understand that the word is mostly irrelevant even as it still retains a great deal of its power. The power comes, I believe, from our inherent understanding of the power of what the word represents.

Still the question remains – what is love? That will be the question I explore in this writing. My latest understanding is simply this: Love is a worldview. It is a way of seeing and perceiving that informs our feelings and our actions, that connects us to all of creation.

Note on Language

For anyone reading this who is not inclined to believe in God, you can substitute the word "Life" or "Consciousness" for "God" without losing the essence of the meaning. Shakespeare said, "That which we call a rose, by any other name would smell as sweet." I say, "That which we call God, by any other name would feel complete."

♥

THANK YOU FOR BREAKING MY HEART

This is the prayer of gratitude I began today with. It was very natural and heartfelt. That, likely, could only be true in the present moment because my heart feels healed right now, having already been broken many times in many ways.

Now it feels broken open, which seems quite different from what most of us normally mean when we talk about "a broken heart." Still, to me it feels like the broken heart I've had in a more conventional sense was a necessary precursor to the current feeling of a broken open heart.

I know for sure that having had my own heart broken in the usual way did bring surprising benefits – only after the overwhelming pain at the time subsided, of course. I certainly never enjoyed it when it was happening, nor was I able in the least to look at things philosophically while in the grip of that pain.

But experiencing the pain that went with the broken

heart definitely made me much more sympathetic toward others in the throes of similar heartache.

It did some other things, too, that I didn't expect. Having a broken heart forced me to look into myself in ways that might never have otherwise occurred to me. Since broken hearts can come from many sources, the first I experienced came long before I had any idea what romantic love was.

My mother left and divorced my father when I was five, taking my younger sister and me to live in a new house and soon with a new dad. My father, Mark, was the one who told me that our family was no longer going to be together. He explained that the split was not my fault or my sister's fault, and that both he and my mother still loved both of us and always would.

In practice, though, over time he grew more and more distant as a wall of broken promises grew between us. To me, it didn't feel like he cared at all anymore, let alone still loved me.

That was my first broken heart.

There were many long-term implications and painful consequences for me, and it's taken decades for me to be able to see the gift that was there for me in that situation. But a gift there was.

These "daddy issues" around abandonment colored much of my young adulthood. I struggled for years with feelings of worthlessness, anger and anxiety over the fear that I was unlovable. Why else would the father I loved and trusted so much reject me the way he had?

I saw within myself all the reasons why. I hated myself for it. I fantasized and yearned to die. I isolated myself from everyone around me, retreating into myself and books to create an impenetrable armor.

This worked to protect me for a long time, but it had an unexpected and unpleasant side effect: it left me alone with someone I hated.

By the time I realized the problem I'd created, my defenses were so high and strong that even I could not defeat them. So I had no other choice than to look more closely at myself.

By then I was in college, living in a dorm far from my family. It had been years since I'd had any contact with Mark, yet I still felt his presence very strongly in my life. I started to wonder about that. How was someone who was absent still able to exert such a strong influence on me? That question forced me to begin to recognize that I was holding him inside myself – or, at least, an image of him I'd made in my mind.

As I thought back over this history of my family, I began to see that Mark himself had been devastated by the breakup of our family. He had retreated into alcoholism and shut himself out of our lives, not unlike what I had done in my own pain. Maybe he was just trying to protect himself, as I was. If that were the case, then maybe it wasn't me he was rejecting, after all. What I did know for sure was that the person hurting me now wasn't him. I only thought it was him because I'd given him that power over me, as if I were still that vulnerable, dependent child who didn't have a choice. I was the one perpetuating the pain.

I made the decision to take that power back and deny him, as well as everyone else, the ability to rule my life. Maybe I couldn't control what other people did or thought, but I could learn to control my own thoughts and actions. I could learn to stop hurting myself with the continuous re-telling of that painful story to myself. If I could just stop doing that, maybe I could let it go and move on.

I resolved not to be a victim anymore, and instead tried to put myself in his shoes when he lost everything he loved. Suddenly, I felt sorry and sad for him, and that compassion allowed me to forgive him. And then I was freed.

This freedom resulted from having my heart broken. The gift from that painful experience was the recognition that I had inside of me a tremendous power to direct my own thoughts and life, in whatever way I choose. By taking responsibility for my own feelings and reactions, I could change them when they weren't working for me, or were hurting me, or holding me back from something I wanted.

That has been a life-changing gift, for which I am eternally grateful. Was it a magical pill that changed everything overnight? No, of course not. But it did eventually affect everything. That decision to take my own power and use it <u>for</u> myself instead of <u>against</u> myself opened my eyes to a new way of being and seeing myself in the world. It was a decision I began to act on again and again. For me, it's been a lifelong practice and something I've had to repeat over and over until it became natural and automatic for me. And, that really has brought a beautiful magic into my life.

So, to Mark and many others who followed: Thank you for breaking my heart. I love you.

WHO IS SPECIAL?

For as long as I can remember, I knew I was different. Something inside of me said, "I am different, I am unique, I am special. Therefore, I deserve love." That sense of my uniqueness has always urged me to resist conformity, yet it also created a sense of disconnection in that I felt that I just didn't "fit in."

Standing apart from the crowd can incur great social costs. Other people often seemed to instinctively sense my standoffishness and usually responded with some version of, "Who do you think you are, that you're better than the rest of us?"

And yet I never once met anyone who said, "I'm just like everyone else and I want to be a clone (or a drone)." No, just the opposite – "I want to feel special."

Here is what I think might be happening. Something deep inside each of us knows, "I am an individual, I am unique, I am (one of) God's chosen one(s)." I am <u>special</u>.

Then the ego hears this, puffs out its chest and declares, "YES! And – the rest of you are NOT."

The ego is very quick to realize, as George Carlin quite hilariously incorporated into his routine, if everyone is special, "the whole idea loses all its fuckin' meaning!"

"I'm special, and you're not" seems to be the driving force in the lives of many of us. Certainly, it's a key reason why so many people around the world insist on monogamy in their long-term relationships and sometimes punish transgressors so harshly. When someone we love shares an intimate connection with another human being, the vast majority of us react violently – emotionally, if not physically, as well – because what could be more threatening to our status as "special"?

It's not just in our romantic relationships that this idea asserts itself. It's a big part of our economy, too. Companies compete to prove how special they and their creations are. Executives and other employees within those companies compete to distinguish themselves as especially valuable. Entire nations jockey for position in the world economy as exceptional. We Americans proclaim explicitly our exceptionalism.

So, what does all of this have to do with love? The first obvious answer is that we all think of those we love as special. If you don't believe your child is special, for example, most people will think there's something wrong with you, feel sorry for your child, and maybe even find ways to punish you as an "unfit" parent.

A less obvious answer might be this: Love

recognizes the ways in which each person is special without destroying the meaning of the word. Love allows you to see that you are special, and, by extension, everyone else is special.

Looking with love, it's clear to me that I am unique, I am special, and I am chosen by God – and if that can be true of me, given everything my ego knows about why I don't deserve it, then why wouldn't the same be true of you, too? In God's eyes, it would. Parents who have more than one child are able quite easily to love each child and to consider each of them special. The specialness of one doesn't make it impossible for any other to be special, whether you have two children or ten. If it did, wouldn't we all just stop after one child? "Sorry, honey, we can't have any more kids because this one is special, so that one available spot for 'special' is already taken." Has anyone ever made that argument?

Love allows us to see what is special about each individual, yet never forces us to restrict our affection and appreciation arbitrarily. This is a paradox that dwells in the realm of God – we can, indeed, ALL be special in our own unique ways without robbing the word of its whole meaning.

♥

GOOD NEWS

"Sure could use a little good news today."[2]

I've definitely been a news junkie at times, and I always keep abreast of current events. This includes listening to talk radio and browsing news sites on the Internet, and I consider myself pretty well informed about political and economic events both at home and abroad.

Few people seem to share that interest. When I've asked, those close to me say they feel overwhelmed. The problems feel hopeless and too complex for any one person to do anything about.

I agree with those assessments at least to some degree. The limitation comes from an understanding that sticking our heads in the sand doesn't solve problems. Ignorance may be bliss, but it's also not very conducive to a strong democracy.

On a deeper level, however, perhaps the opposite

---

[2] "A Little Good News" from the album, *A Little Good News* by Anne Murray.

may be true. There are a lot of good reasons to avoid "news" that hypes and sensationalizes all the worst expressions of humanity. From the perspective of democracy, how helpful can it really be for citizens to hear only about what we dislike or how our systems are failing us, to the point that our small efforts seem like "trying to stop a fire with the moisture from a kiss"?[3]

What is even worse is that all this negativity also forms what psychologists call "social proof" and it tends to actually encourage more of the same. If it seems that everyone's doing it, most people get the idea that it's normal. The problem here is that what the media is always showing us is exactly the opposite of what everyone is actually doing! They do this precisely because it is "newsworthy" (which really just means unusual). And because of the power of mass communication, we all see it and can easily forget that it's nowhere near as pervasive in real life as it is on our screens.

And then there's an even deeper, more dangerous and harder to recognize consequence. All the negativity on our screens goes way beyond just news and includes movies and shows primarily about criminals of one type or another. This focuses our attention, thoughts, and emotions on exactly the things no normal person wants more of in our personal lives.

This aspect of our experience – where we direct our attention, thoughts and emotions – is far more powerful than most of us realize. The power of attraction, as

---

[3] "The Change" from the album, *Fresh Horses* by Garth Brooks.

described in the movie *The Secret*, has been both praised and mocked as delusional New Age garbage. Whatever you think about that, it's worth considering a very practical and even obvious point: the more you think about bad stuff, the worse you feel. Unless you're a psychopath.

One way to think about this world we all share is that it contains all the attributes of <u>both</u> heaven and hell. Whether we think consciously about it or not, we create most of our physical environment. Yes, of course the natural world was already here before us and humans didn't create the planet, but clearly we <u>have</u> created most of the systems and structures we interact with in our daily lives. Most of us in America don't live off the land or sleep under the stars. Most of our children think food comes from supermarkets and have no idea how it gets there. For a lot of adults, our only exposure to nature is human-created landscapes whizzing by and the sun shining brightly through our car windshields.

The point is that <u>we</u> are the primary creators of the world we experience. What we choose to create, and how we do it, depends a lot on whether our thoughts are preoccupied with things we like that bring us joy or things we don't that cause fear. That means the more we focus on attributes of heaven, the more of that we build, and vice versa. When we fear criminals, we build prisons. When we appreciate lush grass and summer breezes, we build parks. You get the idea.

So what are we building more of for ourselves – heaven on Earth, or hell?

Here are some signs that we're building hell:

1. A system of world domination. Even if you ignore the UN, World Bank, IMF, and other so-called global organizations, America itself has built such a system. We don't like to think of ourselves as an empire, but we seem not to mind calling ourselves exceptional, and the sole superpower. While no one knows for sure how many US military bases exist around the world, estimates range from 500 to over 1,000 in some 60+ countries. Less disputed is that US government agencies have a physical presence in 191 countries, complete with armed guards and "276 fortified buildings that comprise the 169 embassies and other missions of the US Department of State."[4]

   If this doesn't qualify as a system of world domination, I don't know what does. Now, this isn't to say America is an "evil empire" abusing its super powers – it may or may not be, but the reality is that the vastness of its capabilities is undeniable. IF it were ever put to evil use, this world would surely be for all practical purposes a living hell for most people.

2. Concentration and isolation of wealth. For those with enough to provide for their needs, this obviously wouldn't be a problem – directly,

---

[4] Julian Assange, *The Wikileaks Files* (London/New York, NY: Verso, 2015), p. 3.

anyway. For everyone else, though, it would be a huge and painful problem. Still, the few who have the wealth tend to separate and isolate themselves from the poor. What that means in practical terms is they lose an opportunity to connect with other people who can enrich their lives in ways that only variety can. They also lose the gifts that loving service to others brings. Helping others and making meaningful contributions to the less fortunate make us feel good and teaches us to appreciate the wonderful things we do have. This is especially true when the contributions are made directly, and not just indirectly (like writing a check). It gives meaning to our lives and relieves the boredom of always getting what we want.

3. Widespread poverty. This is the flip-side of the point above. The more desperate people become just to survive, the more likely they will become a problem for those who do have enough and especially those who seem to have too much. Just imagine all the suffering and death, or take a look at what is actually happening not only in far-off places but even in the heartland. It's heartbreaking.

4. Mass incarceration. America locks up more of its citizens than any other country (based on total number of prisoners overall) and we're a close second on a per capita basis (in percentage terms – behind Seychelles of all

places, and far above any other industrialized country). At best, this is a tremendous waste of human potential and a huge financial cost for taxpayers to bear. It's hard to imagine a clearer sign that we as a society are failing ourselves if we're producing so many people we don't want walking among us.

5. Draconian sentencing. This is related to the previous point, of course, but it also indicates a certain vindictiveness, a lack of willingness to help lost folks get back on track, and a refusal to deal with the root causes of the problem in the first place. Strike, you're out! Welcome to hell, where second chances and forgiveness are nowhere to be found.

6. Even for minor violations. It would be bad enough to punish harshly only those guilty of horrific crimes, but we go way beyond even that. It isn't only violent criminals serving decades-long or even life sentences. We also throw away people who are mentally ill, addicted to various drugs, and otherwise generally non-violent individuals who simply don't live how we want them to. Some of them have hurt nobody other than themselves. If you can be stripped of your humanity and forced to live in a cage because we don't like your race, or poverty, or some other aspect of your life, you are probably living in hell.

7. Climate destruction. Fires, floods, hurricanes, tornadoes, earthquakes and other similar natural disasters surely belong to hell, not heaven. If you argue these are acts of God with no human component of responsibility, here's another menu for you: contaminated and poisoned water that will give you cancer or in some places even catch on fire (water catching on fire! Now there's a hellish image for you), air blackened by belching smoke to breathe (not just in Beijing), and "food" filled with fat and sugar but no nutrition to eat. A lot more could be said, but that alone is already as clear a description of hell as you probably need.

8. Ecosystem destruction. This is related to but not the same as climate destruction. We aren't just poisoning and killing off ourselves, we're sharing that generously with the rest of our planet's inhabitants. We've already sent a lot of species the way of the Dodo and so far we aren't stopping.

9. Deficient healthcare. Our profit-motivated medical system has a lot of customers and not a lot of interest in real cures. Wellness doesn't drive up the stock prices of Big Pharma and empty hospital beds don't send doctors to the Bahamas on vacation. Like most of the points before this, the key thing to understand here is that the problem is how the system is designed

to work and not the individual people who work as cogs within it.

10. Lack of access to education. Education offers a path out of hell because it teaches you how to think, especially about non-obvious things like how systems work. Why would the overlords of hell want anyone to understand how they got there and why, if that holds the key to them figuring out how to get out? Without education, people can be duped a lot more easily into just going along with the way things are.

11. Wars and Weapons of Mass Destruction. This might be so obvious it needs no explanation. Murder and mayhem on a mass scale must belong in the realm of hell.

This is not an exhaustive list. We are well on our way to creating hell on Earth.

Now, let's take a deep breath and turn away from all of that toward the brighter side of the coin.

Here are some signs that we're building heaven:
1. Organized governance. This just refers to a structure for managing our interactions with one another. It isn't only about government at the largest scale, but does include it. We are social animals and the actions of an individual can affect others, so we need a way to manage and resolve conflicts (other than just

killing each other when we disagree). At its best, this is what government does. It's really just a set of agreements we make about how we treat each other and what to do if we think we've been mistreated. This covers everything from global-scale interactions down to the communities we live in, the places where we work, and even our families. Ultimately we're looking to make agreements that work to foster cooperation, ideally with as little loss of individual freedom as possible.

We humans have done a lot to create structures that support working together in productive ways and minimizing violence. Some work better than others and we don't all always agree about where to draw the lines dividing what's OK from what's not, but we have come a long way from the chaos of the jungle.

2. Organized means of production. When a lot of people live close together, we need a lot of resources to provide for the means of survival (think food, water, clothing, shelter, etc.) and an efficient and reasonably equitable way to share them. We've done a pretty good job figuring out how to produce and access not only the things we need, but also what we want. This is a major accomplishment when you consider everything that goes into it and all the different and competing desires people

have. We've created a lot of things that make life much easier for us, not to mention fun and pleasant in all kinds of ways. We have gotten very good at finding ways to provide for ourselves and, even if there are ways we could do even better, our resourcefulness has solved a lot of problems that used to vex and kill our ancestors.

3. Appreciation for innovation. We humans are a very smart and creative species, and we've grown to really value our ability to make things better as we define that. Overall we're pretty open to experimenting and trying out new ideas in pretty much all aspects of life. We're always pushing for more and better, and this forward striving to grow keeps raising the bar in ways that excite and challenge us.

4. Efforts at global cooperation. We've gotten so good at working together at more local levels that now we're even working toward achieving it at the global scale. We increasingly see ourselves as part of a single world, even with all our beautiful variations. We seem to understand that the better we make things for everyone, the better off each of us individually can be. At a minimum, we recognize that reducing conflict on the broadest scale (war, etc.) can free up a lot of energy we can use to get more of the good things we want.

5. Doing our best. If heaven by definition represents the best of everything we can imagine, then a sure sign we're heading in that direction is when we ourselves are trying to do our best. It could be about anything, really, as long as we are motivated to give our best effort at something we care about. This is different from trying to be "the best" out of everyone at something. That would qualify, of course, but doing your best is more about reaching for the highest heights you currently have the ability, energy, skills, commitment and desire to attain. Accordingly, your best will be different from anyone else's and even from your own best at a different time. Reaching for it is what makes it a sign of heaven because you probably wouldn't bother in hell.

6. Music and art exist! These pursuits are not a physical necessity for most of us – though they must surely arise from the deepest yearnings of our souls for beauty and joyful expression. In many ways our culture puts a high value on music and art, considering how much the most successful artists and entertainers can earn for their work (here I would also include athletes, because at their best sports are a physical art). Amateurs also love to engage in these activities, and their prevalence in a culture in general both reflects and contributes to a tangible vision of heaven.

7. Strong communication network. This network represents our literal connection of each one of us to every other. It allows us to share ideas and evidence of best practices in solving difficult problems. This kind of sharing (and the very system that allows it) is a bedrock of heaven, even if some among us choose to abuse it. We can all participate in sharing our visions for the kind of world we'd like to live in, and hopefully create a shared vision we're willing to work together to bring into reality. What wonders might we make?

8. Good travel network. Our planet is quickly becoming one interconnected world. In addition to being able to talk with people across the globe, we can physically go and connect in person, too, within just a few hours. This has never before been possible and although not everyone can presently access this opportunity, as the network continues to grow and prices come down it will just keep getting easier.

9. Intentional improvement. As individuals and collectively, we care a lot about improving everything from the condition of our physical surroundings to the quality of our relationships to our personal effectiveness in the world. There is always something we can identify as lacking or undesirable and we want it to get better. Regardless of how much effort and

commitment you might be willing to put into making changes, you can probably think of at least five things off the top of your head right now that you're wanting or working to improve. If not, you're probably taking some kind of medication, legal or otherwise, to treat depression (or some other ailment). And if you are depressed, as so many Americans sadly are, that's probably caused at least in part by the difference between what your life is actually like and how you thought it would be when you were younger. Still, the only reason to take pills, powder or alcohol is because you want to feel better. The desire for continuous improvement is heaven-sent.

10. Entrepreneurial attitude. We Americans are deeply committed to the ideas of free enterprise, self-reliance, and capitalism as an economic engine to create prosperity. Small businesses provide a lot of jobs and self-employment is a strong and growing source of income for a lot of people. This is a natural outgrowth from a "can-do" attitude, and our optimism, especially perhaps when others see it as baseless, propels us to ever greater heights despite the risks involved. This is very closely tied to faith, of course, and we admire those who persist through sheer determination to build what did not exist before. This willingness to shake things up and attempt the heretofore "impossible" is an aspect of freedom

and creation that could only come from heaven.

This list is no more complete than the previous one, although I confess it was quite a bit more difficult and significantly more fun to compile. We have also been making some great strides toward creating heaven on Earth.

Right now, the most important question is: Which list do you want to help expand? This is no idle or rhetorical question. Every human being on the planet is a co-creator in this world we all share, consciously or not, willingly or not, powerfully or not. Part of how you participate is determined by your physical actions, of course. Some people seek to serve others, while others are more focused on taking for themselves. Some spend a lot of time thinking about these questions, while others put every last ounce of energy into just staying alive (and a few, tragically, give up even trying).

Wherever you find yourself on the spectrum, the other way you participate in this co-creation is through your thoughts and feelings. How you choose to direct your attention – and that is a choice, and one that nobody else can ever make for you – shapes your attitude, your mood, and your willingness to engage in the game of life. If you choose to withdraw, it means that your voice and your vote go toward continuing things exactly as they are now.

What do you think could happen if you put a small amount of effort into making a more active choice to focus your attention on good news or ignore the bad?

This is a very practical way to incorporate love more fully into our daily lives. Maybe we all could use a little good news today.

♥

THE QUALITY OF OUR THOUGHTS DETERMINES THE QUALITY OF OUR LIVES

One of Leo Tolstoy's lesser known quotes, especially in English, is this: "Thoughts are key. Everything begins as a thought. And thoughts can be directed. Therefore, working on thoughts is the most important part of improvement."[5] I ran across this last summer in a bookshop in St. Petersburg, Russia (I lived in that beautiful city for 6 years and this was my first time back in almost a decade).

The truth of that statement struck me immediately so I bought the magnet it was printed on. Magnetic philosophy! Profound insight can come from anywhere, even cheap silly trinkets apparently.

This idea about the power of thoughts is something

---

[5] Leo Tolstoy, *Selected Journals* published in Russian, entry dated June 26, 1899.

I've seen repeated in many different places. Despite having experienced examples of it working for me personally on plenty of occasions in my own life, I've felt a lot of resistance to actively embracing it and for a long time had a sort of love-hate relationship to it. I'm not even really sure why, other than how trite it often sounds. Change your thoughts, change your life. The power of positive thinking. These phrases from book titles and others like them have permeated our culture and spawned entire sub-cultures. Maybe they seem too simplistic to be taken seriously. Still, profound truth is surprisingly often quite simple (or simple-sounding). Could that be why some of us think them simple-minded?

Yet simple is far from the same as easy. Sometimes the simplest things can be the hardest to do, like eating healthy food and getting a good night's sleep.

Thoughts can include the chatter we hear in our heads as background noise as well as more focused attention on some problem we may be trying to solve. The second type of thought feels more important and meaningful because it usually results in some plan of action. This, in turn, leads to concrete steps that create visible change. Compared to actions, thoughts can seem pretty useless.

Tolstoy's reminder that "everything begins as a thought" points to an easily overlooked part of the creative process. A thought is like a seed. All ideas are thoughts, and not all of them sprout or grow. Without them, nothing grows.

We all know that higher quality seeds produce higher quality plants, and if the quality of a seed is poor it might not produce anything at all. For some reason very few of us apply the same logic to our thoughts. Why is that?

Maybe there's a problem with the analogy. For one thing, seeds and plants are both physical things and thoughts are not. And if we liken thoughts to seeds, what is the corresponding equivalent to plants? Presumably it would be whatever is manifested in the physical world, whether a thing invented or a particular behavior. And an action or behavior can be considered a physical thing because it's observable by our eyes. In other words, it's a lot easier to believe and accept that a physical cause has a physical effect (seed to plant) than it is to recognize that a non-physical cause has a physical effect. Yet thoughts <u>do</u> affect reality.

Quality is a subjective judgment. Is something good enough – for a particular purpose or to meet a certain standard? "Quality" can refer to a distinctive characteristic that describes something and it can also mean excellence. If you look honestly you'll probably find a high correlation between the quality of your thoughts and the quality of your life in both senses of the word. If your level of satisfaction with your life is low, it's a pretty safe bet that your thoughts (and even the words you speak out loud) are laced with complaints and criticism. On the other hand, if you feel things are going well for you, you probably also think (and talk) quite a bit about things you consider good.

If you struggle with frustration because it's hard to make ends meet financially, look to see how often you're thinking about all the things you don't have. If it seems like you always get the rude cashier or someone steals the parking spot you were just about to pull into, pay some attention to how much anger colors your thoughts with rehashed conversations with someone who annoys you. And if an old friend you were thinking about the other day calls you out of the blue just because they miss you, consider how often your thoughts about others are fond and warm. This will probably be quite easy.

Now try the reverse. If someone cut you off on the freeway and almost ran you off the road, check how often you think about the random kindness of strangers. If you won $50 on a scratcher, consider how often you tell yourself that nothing ever goes your way. Did you notice any patterns? If you found it more difficult to link your thoughts and experiences in this exercise than in the last one, consider it a telling illustration of how thoughts relate to reality.

Correlation is not causation and when you look at these things it can seem like a chicken-and-egg problem to figure out which is cause and which is effect, or even if there's any connection at all. This is where science helps, but maybe not in the way you think. Look at the research if you want, but in the meantime you can try your own experiment. Since events can be so hard to control, try controlling your thoughts instead. There are lots of ways to start. Here are some that have worked for me:

- As soon as possible after waking up, say to yourself, "I expect to have a good day today."
- Smile at least 10 times during the day
- Listen to your favorite music on the way to work

- If something upsets you, take a deep breath and shift your focus to something pleasant for 30 seconds
- Try to imagine what the other person might be thinking, or what you might think and do in their shoes

♥

"YOU CAN'T TEACH AN OLD DOG NEW TRICKS"

Here's a piece of conventional wisdom that a lot of people apparently believe, at least to some degree. But why can't you teach an old dog new tricks?

I doubt it's because the older ones are simply less able than the young or have forgotten how to learn. More likely they tend to be less open to new things and less willing to put in the effort required to learn something well. But there's probably more to it than that.

Three powerful factors can get in the way of that openness and willingness to change (and learning can be seen as an aspect of change). They are:

1. Neurological factors – how the brain is wired and operates
2. Attachment factors – how we become familiar and comfortable emotionally with what we already know

3. Identity factors – how we see ourselves as "just the way I am"

Neurological Factors

Scientists have learned a great deal in the past decade or two about how our brains work. There's still plenty we don't know, to be sure, but some key discoveries are relevant here. Our brain is made up of cells called neurons, and these neurons are constantly communicating with one another. The right hand may not know what the left is doing, but in normal people the brain does know what both are doing and it also usually knows why. That's because these neurons share information across what we can think of as a "brain superhighway." These pathways between neurons are created in a way similar to how footpaths through the forest are created – the more often electrical impulses travel between any two neurons, the easier it becomes to travel that path. It's more like building bridges than clearing a path, actually, and the tissues in the brain will reflect these well-worn paths over time by continuing to strengthen those connections.

At the same time, unsurprisingly, other pathways that don't get used so much tend to remain undeveloped. Think about the difference between an unpaved service road that's been washed out and has a lot of potholes compared to a major interstate highway, and you have a fairly decent representation of what neural pathways in the brain are like. Some are much easier to travel than others.

Repetition is what creates the stronger pathways,

which is why habits can be so hard to break – they represent a sort of default for the brain. It's also why experienced drivers can get around basically on autopilot. If you're on a road you often use but not going where you normally do, you can easily take a wrong but familiar turn if your mind has wandered, precisely for this reason. So this ability of the brain to automate repeated tasks saves us a lot of effort and trouble by reducing how much we need to concentrate to get anything done. Unfortunately, it also means that change requires a lot of conscious effort in the beginning. Like the young, older dogs (and people) have to focus at first on what they're trying to do that they haven't done before. But they also have to override the default of what they've gotten used to in the past. That's probably why I'm having a hard time getting a couple five-year-old animals to start to use the pet door we just put in, especially since it's a different door on the other side of the house than they're used to. They just keep going to the door they've always used!

Attachment

If neurology is "I've gotten used to it," attachment is "I like it this way." Even if you don't particularly like it, the familiar is comforting and easy. What's not to like about that?! The devil we know is preferable to the one we don't.

Most of us form very strong attachments to people, places, pets, hobbies, sports teams, or whatever. How inclined are you to give up any of those? The more you've invested emotionally, the more you'll resist letting go of an attachment because the pain of loss is so much greater. Research also confirms that we tend to care a lot more about avoiding loss and pain than we do about gaining benefits and joy. This fact helps to make sense of why people will resist even positive changes, including in extreme cases like battered wives staying with their abusers.

As adults, learning something new, especially when it comes to how we see and think about ourselves or the world around us, often means giving up what we're already doing and have gotten used to. And there's almost always something we like about that, even if it's just the predictability of familiarity. We can be attached to it simply because we know it well, whether it works best for us or not.

Identity

When we internalize habits and customs that have been passed down to us from our families and culture, they become a part of our identity. This can include everything from rituals (religion, holidays, etc.) to expectations (ideas about who we are and how to be in relation to the world). Most often, these aspects of identity are transmitted and adopted without a lot of conscious thought and perhaps even less (perceived) room for personal decision-making. They can even feel inevitable because "that's just the way things are." We learn what it means to be any given race, religion, nationality, etc. from the people we know and see who are also part of the same identity group. Rejecting or perhaps merely challenging these notions is hard because it's more than a purely personal choice that affects the individual making the decision. Maybe that's one reason why so much of this cultural learning happens intensely in childhood. Children are usually in no position to choose, and by the time they're old enough to be capable of making such choices they've already had years of training in how to be a good _____ (insert race, religion, nationality, etc.). They're invested very heavily in that identity.

The momentum these three forces produce is powerful, especially because there are often many mechanisms in place to discourage deviation. Neurology favors the well-worn path and sustained effort is necessary to create new ones. The bonds of attachment provide emotional rewards in return for maintaining existing connections (like a comforting habit). And social acceptance in our identity groups pays off with lots of dividends like help in finding jobs and mates. Leaving these things behind to try something new comes with a cost, sometimes a very steep one. The old dog likes his spot on the pillow, so why get up to chase a ball?! And if it's a laser instead of a ball, there's nothing even there to catch!

And yet despite all of this, we can and sometimes do overcome the barriers by following a deeper and more powerful drive to be free. Free to be me, as the best version of myself I can imagine.

If that vision of my best self matches my existing habits, attachments, and identity, then I don't need to look any further than where I am now. Trouble is, I can't think of any time when that's been true in my experience. How about you? Beyond that, it sounds to me like an end to growth, which is stagnation at best and the decay of death at worst. Not appealing!

One of my all-time favorite quotes has always been this by e.e. cummings: "To be nobody but yourself, in a world which is doing its best, night and day, to make you everybody else, means to fight the hardest battle which any human being can fight, and never stop fighting." Committing to being your best self is a powerful act of love.

Yet habits, attachments and identity can often feel like a prison imposed on us by others. The truth is that it may have started that way, but most often it becomes self-imposed. It's like the old story of training an elephant baby by tying it with a rope to a pole. The baby can't break the rope. When it grows up, it's tied to the pole with a chain. The adult elephant has more than enough strength to break the chain but it never even tries, because it's already learned that it can't. What kinds of chains hold us back from what we want and who we could be if we simply tried to break them?

COMPARING TO CRITICIZE

Is there anyone out there who has never compared themselves to someone else? Doubtful. Have you ever noticed that when you make these kinds of comparisons, more often than not the result is that you feel worse rather than better about yourself? For me that was overwhelmingly true and it started very early in life.

As I've already mentioned, I have a younger sister and I can't imagine a richer soil for comparisons than same-gender siblings. In our family the labels broke down essentially to "the smart one" and "the social one" but it didn't end there. We also knew who was "the skinny one" – clearly implying its opposite, "the fat one" – and who was "the obedient one" – again, implying its corollary, "the troublesome one" – and so on. I think we both felt it all really meant "the good one" and "the bad one" – and we both felt like "the bad one."

It wasn't a case of all positive attributes lining up in

one person and negative ones in the other. It might seem weird, then, that we both felt "less than" in a generalized way not limited to any particular yardstick. I've had a lot of conversations about this with my sister and I don't presume to speak for her here, but I think it's safe to say we both suffered from feelings of inferiority arising from these kinds of comparisons. "Winning" one never felt like enough to compensate for being a "loser" in another.

Why do people compare themselves and others in this way? The only value I see in comparisons among people is that sometimes the only way to recognize what you are is to identify what you're not. I'm not sure that value is worth the cost in painful feelings of inadequacy. Maybe the problem isn't with the comparison itself, but instead with how and why we do it.

Starting with the question of why, I have no idea what motivated adults in our family to draw the comparisons they did about my sister and me, but I don't believe it was anything intentionally malicious. I compared myself to my sister mostly because that's what I saw others doing and probably also because she was the person closest to my age in close physical proximity. Where parents and other adults are concerned, even if the intention in making comparisons is not to hurt, it probably isn't really kindness, either. Often, I felt others were comparing to criticize or even to manipulate. "Why can't you be more like...?" is a question I bet we've all heard at one time or another. When you did hear it, it was undoubtedly clear that you were being judged by comparison and found lacking.

This brings us to the issue of how comparisons are made. Why is it that we focus primarily on comparing people to those who are "better" in some way, and not the other way around? It would be so much nicer to hear, "I'm really glad you get your homework and chores done right after school instead of waiting until bedtime to start like I used to do at your age." Not only does that kind of comparison reinforce a positive behavior to the listener, it also avoids putting down someone else for their current behavior.

"Keeping up with the Joneses" is, of course, one of the best-known types of comparisons we make. Just its phrasing communicates clearly that these mythical "Joneses" are much better off and thus represent an ideal worth striving toward. We know nothing about them, though, except that they have more money and stuff than us, and we're lagging behind. We have no idea whether the Joneses are kind or cruel, generous or stingy, friendly or hostile, ethical people or criminals. None of that matters – in this comparison, you will lose. By definition they're more fortunate than you regardless of whatever good you have going for you. Any comparison with these Joneses will leave you feeling bad about yourself.

Comparing ourselves with those who are worse off than us, by contrast, is something we rarely do. The only one that comes immediately to mind is when someone says, "Eat everything on your plate. Don't you know there are children starving in Africa?!" This one is steeped in guilt and manages also to make us feel bad about ourselves. Talk about a no-win situation! Feeling worse off by comparison breeds envy – an emotion that's completely incompatible with love. And a comparison used specifically to make you feel guilty about being better off than someone else is hardly better – guilt also crowds out love. And it obscures gratitude for good fortune, which actually is an expression of love.

Some readers might be thinking, "So what? What do I care whether people I don't even know feel good about themselves or not?" We all have our own issues to concern ourselves with and the feelings of a random stranger are down pretty low on that list of priorities. At least until he opens fire with a military-style weapon at the neighborhood school. Or sells you shares in a Ponzi scheme that wipes out your life savings. Or finds some other way to take out his frustration and rage on everyone unlucky enough to cross his path that day. It could be today or tomorrow, and any of us could suffer for being in the wrong place at the wrong time. On the other hand, people who feel good about themselves tend not to harm others and themselves in the many ways you can hear about on the nightly news.

It should go without saying that none of this means the actions of a disturbed individual are the fault of their family, friends, co-workers, religious affiliation, race, etc. All of us are responsible for our own actions, words, feelings, thoughts, and so on. None of them occur in a vacuum, however, and the way we treat one another makes a difference. It has a ripple effect. And we are all responsible, together, for our cultural norms, attitudes, and expectations. A society is only as healthy as the people who live in it. From that perspective, it matters a lot whether we choose to complain, compare and criticize one another and ourselves. We could instead choose to adopt a more loving attitude, sharing generously our support, appreciation, and praise to help one another see the best in ourselves. Which will you choose today?

♥

THINKING ABOUT RELATIONSHIPS

Who do you dislike? Go ahead and make a list, then count how many names are on it. Put a mark next to the name of every person who is either 1) a member of your immediate family (including parents and siblings), or 2) someone you interact with regularly (more often than once a week). Next to each name, write down the one thing that is the sharpest thorn in your side, the person's worst quality. Now consider each person for up to 30 seconds to determine how often you think about this fault of theirs – is it multiple times every day with extended conversations in your head, or maybe a couple times a month in passing, or somewhere else on the intensity spectrum?

Now shift gears. Consider each person again, and this time write down their three best qualities – and a specific example of each based on your personal experience with that person.

Now just take a moment to notice which exercise

was easier. It's obvious, you might say, because we started with people I dislike! Yes – because this was about recognizing just how much practice you've had with dwelling on one side of the coin while ignoring the other. Now do the same thing in reverse (listing people you like and their one best quality and so on), especially if you felt cheated by this little thought experiment. Taken together, these exercises should give you a fairly accurate sense of how much of your thinking is negative and how much is positive. It may also have given you some insight into the quality of your relationships as you see them. By now you can probably anticipate the next link: how we think about the people in our lives has a profound influence on how well we get along with them. This, in turn, is the driving force behind how we evaluate the quality of our lives.

You might be skeptical about this idea that how you think about someone causes the problems in your relationship. Maybe you think your opinions of people are based on what you see them saying and doing, and all you're doing is drawing conclusions based on evidence. Your boss is a jerk, for example, or your teenager is lazy, and you're not the only one who thinks so.

That may be true. Yet it's probably not the whole truth. There are aspects of every situation, just as there are with every human being, that could be called heavenly or hellish, good or bad, things you like and those you don't. Which among them you pay more attention to can depend on a lot of things, like whether you're dependent on them for something, what else is going on in your life at the moment, your mood today, even what the weather is like. What you think of someone in general also matters.

Psychologists have identified a phenomenon called "confirmation bias" and it has a subtle but important effect on not just how we interpret things but also what we notice. It basically means we tend to see what we expect and give a lot more weight and significance to evidence that confirms what we already believe is true. Along with that, we also tend to discount evidence that contradicts what we think is true. A simple example might be that we think the sky is blue so we notice when it has that deep azure color. We might also call someone argumentative – like my parents did in exasperation with me! – when they point out that the sky actually has no color at all and objectively some other color most of the time (e.g., black at night, gray when overcast, red, orange and purple at sunset, etc.). In our relationships with other people, though, confirmation bias can lead us to see only the worst in someone if we've already decided they're unreliable, selfish, a gossip, a liar, or any other negative judgment we might make.

This tendency plays out in our public life, as well. For example, political pundits frequently excoriate politicians of the other party for saying or doing something they previously defended when done by a member of their preferred party. This just illustrates how we can often go to great lengths to interpret in a positive light the words, actions, and even presumed intentions of someone we're inclined favorably toward and vice versa. We give the benefit of the doubt to people we like and think well of, and assume the worst of those we don't. This is confirmation bias in action.

Knowing this, we can turn it to our advantage in improving our personal relationships with everyone around us. The way to do it is very simple: shift your focus away from what you don't like and toward what you do.

I referred earlier to "heavenly" and "hellish" attributes of people and situations because both inevitably exist and the choice of which to focus on will determine where you "live" in relationship to that person or situation. Most of the time these decisions are made without much conscious thought about how it affects us emotionally to see someone or something in a particular way. It may even seem that making such a conscious choice is silly or inauthentic. Choosing to see the best can get you ridiculed as a "Pollyanna" – as if that were actually a bad thing! Choosing to see the worst normally won't cause other people to mock you, although if you do it often and overtly enough they might start to avoid you. Regardless, whether you've thought much about it or not, you are making a choice. Choosing one way or the other has likely become a habit for you. And that habit is a much more powerful influence on the nature of your relationships with other people than you might realize.

I know for sure that improving my own relationships with family members and even myself has never been possible without first changing my mind about the other person. Changing the way I thought about them in turn changed how I talked and acted around them. For example, my sister and I used to fight like cats and dogs when we were kids. That's pretty normal among siblings but we saw ourselves as so different from each other and got along so badly that we basically had no relationship with each other at all by the time we were teenagers. I can't say what she thought of me, but I felt pretty sure she hated me. I thought of her as vain, selfish, uncaring, and superficial.

One day after I'd turned 18 and was preparing to leave for college, I was feeling really emotional and started to cry softly. My sister noticed and, to my surprise, asked what was wrong. Maybe because I felt I had nothing to lose, I told her the truth about my anxiety over leaving as well as my sense that she didn't care about me at all. If my thinking about that had been correct, though, she never would have asked the question in the first place! And the conversation that followed proved how very wrong I had been. If I had just brushed her off in my conviction that she didn't care anyway, I have no idea how that would have turned out but certainly very differently than it did. If I had been unwilling to change the way I thought about my sister, I would have missed out on the best friend I've ever had. I would have lost the most trusted and loyal confidante of my life. I would have been unable to learn from the differences I knew and the similarities I discovered. If I'm completely honest, I doubt I would even be here today. The hardest and most challenging relationships in my life have all turned out to be the greatest gifts, best teachers, and closest bonds I've experienced. I only know that because I was willing to change the way I thought about the people in those relationships.

Here are some simple steps to improve any

relationship:

1. Open a willingness to <u>listen</u>
2. Practice <u>listening</u>!
3. Ask questions to <u>understand</u>
4. Deal with the person <u>directly</u>
5. Tell the truth from your perspective in a gentle and respectful way

♥

FORGIVENESS IS THE ONLY PATH TO PEACE

Some people are able to forgive even in extreme circumstances while others will hold a grudge for years over what might seem to outsiders like a small slight. Two examples: one involves the death penalty and the other is an incident I remember from childhood.

The use of the death penalty in the United States has always been controversial, and recent problems with lethal injections have brought the disagreements back into the public debate. Supporters of the death penalty often speak publicly about a desire to protect the rights of victims and their families as a reason to keep execution legal. Yet the family members of murder victims sometimes line up with the opposition, pointing out in such cases that executing a murderer will not bring their loved one back. Some go so far as to profess publicly their forgiveness for the murderer of their loved one. It's hard to imagine a case more extreme than forgiving someone for killing your spouse, parent, or child. Yet it happens.

At the other end of the spectrum, I remember an incident that happened around the time when I was eight years old. My mom and her relatively new husband, my sister, and I were driving in our car behind my grandparents (my mom's parents) to their new home, located about an hour away from where we lived. The plan was to spend the weekend together in this largely undeveloped part of California where the night sky shone with countless breathtaking stars. The route included a steep grade where cars often overheated (this was in the 70s) and there was little opportunity around to seek help. At the top of the grade our car broke down and dad, despite his best efforts, was unable to get it running again. My grandparents stopped with us, but their two-seater truck certainly wouldn't fit four more people even to go the last 10 miles.

My grandfather was a AAA member and entitled to free roadside assistance, but my parents were not. My grandfather refused dad's request to use his membership on our behalf, on the grounds that he could only call for help twice a year and if he used it now, it wouldn't be available if he needed it in the future. He also asserted that dad should have had his own membership or other means of providing for his family himself. Dad was livid and outraged that grandpa would not even agree to help his daughter by rescuing her with her two small children when he had the means to do so easily.

That argument ruined the weekend – both men told

each other to go to hell and after the car was repaired dad turned around and drove us home. And the two of them refused to speak to each other for the next seven years, ruining many more weekends and holidays along the way. Their stubborn refusal to forgive or even try to see the situation from the other's point of view caused a lot of trouble and heartache not just for them, but the whole extended family.

Although I was a child when it happened, I learned a lot from that experience. Looking back now almost four decades later, it's clear to me that they were both right, and both wrong. My grandfather had thought ahead about how to handle an unexpected challenge and purchased a sort of insurance, and he wanted to keep it available in case he needed it rather than give it to someone who hadn't been so responsible in planning for contingencies. From his perspective, it was no longer his responsibility to take care of his daughter; it was her husband's. From my dad's perspective, it was selfish and stingy to refuse to help when doing so would have been free and easy. Particularly in light of the fact that my grandpa was a devout Catholic, it felt like a very uncharitable and even un-Christian way to behave. Ultimately both were so caught up in the righteousness of their positions that they were unable to see past their own noses.

Forgiveness can be very difficult, particularly when issues of morality are involved or we hold strong opinions about what is right or wrong. We are a lot more inclined to forgive actions that hurt us inadvertently or to a relatively low degree – like someone stepping on your toes in a crowded place –

than when we perceive the harmful action to be intentional or the cause of serious harm. No surprise there but – you guessed it – the critical factor is how we think about and interpret what happened.

Forgiveness requires a willingness to look beyond our own naturally limited point of view. It springs from acceptance of a situation or person as they are, as opposed to a resistance based on what we'd prefer them to be. This acceptance or resistance in turn reflects our own sense of inner strength and personal power in light of what we're facing. Fear and a sense of powerlessness or weakness leads to resistance, frustration, and anger because we see ourselves as helpless to change an unsatisfactory situation (or person, for that matter). Anger is a natural response when we don't know how to handle a frustrating situation and forgiveness is all but impossible in the heat of it. Acceptance, on the other hand, derives from inner strength and conviction that we can handle it, either by changing it or letting it go so it's not a threat we need to worry about. When we look at something that way, it diminishes in power and influence over us, allowing in the possibility of forgiveness.

Acceptance and forgiveness are sometimes confused with condoning something. To this way of thinking, forgiving someone for a wrong they've done to us is to "let them get away with it" and perhaps even encourage them to do it again. Not so.

If you see it as your job to judge and punish others, not only do you put an undue burden on yourself but you virtually guarantee that you will never live in peace. Moreover, you misunderstand who truly benefits from forgiveness or suffers from condemnation. Forgiveness is a gift we give to <u>ourselves</u> because we are the ones who live every day with our own feelings. Thus when we forgive, we simply release ourselves from our own bad feelings. Forgiveness is an affirmation of our power to choose our own state of mind, regardless of external events. In this way, it also affirms our power to refuse to allow others to hurt us, making it much easier to avoid feeling victimized and effectively stop the continuation of offensive or otherwise unacceptable behaviors toward us. This works because it allows us to respond from a position of power, not weakness.

Love is the springboard that enables us to "jump the tracks" from weakness and resistance to power and acceptance. If love is a certain way of looking at the world, as I believe it is, then it is a type of filter for perception. Looking through the lens of love, we can see a more complete picture that includes virtues as well as faults. By expanding our perspective this way, we can begin to imagine ourselves in the shoes of another person and acknowledge that their perspective may also be valid. Even if we're convinced that we'd make a better choice in the same situation, we might also consider the possibility that at another time in our lives we might have done something that affected someone else similarly to how we're feeling now. Love is what makes it possible for us to relate to one another at all, and recognizing some aspect of ourselves in another person has a powerful effect.

Ideally we might hope that relating in this way would make us feel closer and more forgiving, but in truth it can also go the other way. If we recognize and relate to a quality in them that we fear or despise in ourselves, that can cause resistance or denial, and further entrenchment as I suspect may have happened in the case with my dad and grandpa.

This is a sad case in which forgiveness is especially needed yet seems out of reach. First we must forgive ourselves for our perceived imperfections. If you have something inside yourself that you don't like or can't accept, the best way I know to get unstuck from that is to own it so you can use it. Use it how? To define its opposite, a vision that reflects what you do like and would willingly accept in yourself. That vision represents a part of you that must exist if you can think of it and it can show itself through your behavior if you choose for it to. When you hold that vision in mind, however contrary you may think it is to what you may have long secretly feared was the real truth about yourself, you are beginning to identify yourself with a different part of you that matches the way you'd like to be.

Persisting in that way pays off. As you let go of the old to embrace the new, you feel good about yourself. Letting go is forgiveness.

Once applied to yourself and accepted, forgiveness naturally reaches out to others. It can be other aspects of yourself and other people. That's because you are beginning to see and act in a new way. When you see results that please you, the desire to continue simply grows. Forgiveness – letting go – brings peace, and peace is a valuable blessing!

I IDENTIFY WITH ATHEISTS AS MUCH AS WITH CHRISTIANS

"Schizophrenic" may be the first word that comes to mind when you read the sentence that is this chapter's heading. I've said that I've believed in God since I was very young and that I've also turned away from the religions I've known so therein lies the basis for this statement.

As I see it, religion and science use two different languages to talk about the same thing. From that perspective there's no contradiction between them. Science uses a language of rationality and reason, which can be likened to the prose of a textbook or other academic treatise. Religion uses poetry, a language of feeling and emotion, perhaps like a Shakespearean sonnet. Shakespeare and scientists may describe the sun differently but that neither means one is wrong nor that they're referring to two separate objects.

It makes no sense to approach poetry the same way as an academic text, yet it seems many religious people attempt to do exactly that when it comes to their holy books (whether the *Bible*, *Koran*, *Torah*, *Bhagavad Gita* or whatever other they hold dear). It is not necessary for a story to be literally and factually accurate in all its details for its essence to be true. In fact, communication of difficult or confusing concepts can sometimes be improved and clarified immensely through skilled use of storytelling devices, and many of our best-known enlightened masters used parables and other such methods to teach and share knowledge. Interpreting such stories in too literal a way can actually obscure and limit understanding of the ideas being conveyed.

I'll share a favorite parable I heard many years ago that struck me powerfully:

An old man was walking slowly along a road leading to and from a great city behind him. A young man with a knapsack came upon the old man and said to him, "I see that you are coming from the city there ahead of me. I have collected my things and gone out from my home to seek my fortune in life. Tell me, please, what are the people like in that city there?" The old man considered a moment before replying, "Tell me, what are the people like in the place you're from?" The young man responded enthusiastically, "Oh, they are so kind and generous! I miss my family and village terribly yet I must continue my journey and I hope to make them proud." The old man said, "You'll find them much the same in the city ahead." The young traveler smiled, thanked the old man, and went on.

A short time later the old man encountered another traveler on the same road into the city. Again he was stopped and asked the same question. The traveler explained, "You see, I'm off to seek my fortune. The town where I grew up has no opportunities for me. Everyone is concerned only for themselves and won't lift a finger to help another. They sure do gossip, though! I'm glad to be out of there because the people are so awful." The old man thought a moment and said, "I'm afraid you'll find them much the same in the city ahead."

Does this parable need to describe factually accurate events to share a great truth about the power of expectations? I think not.

Reading the story and applying a literal interpretation, you will quickly see that it's meaningless and the old man is just a crazy schizophrenic detached from reality. There's nothing more to say about it.

Reading it in a more poetic mindset, however, reveals many layers of meaning. It can be seen to point to profound ideas such as:

1. We tend to find whatever it is we're paying attention to or looking for
2. What we think about people and the world shapes how we look and what we find
3. Everything is already there, whether we can see it or not
4. What to seek is a personal choice
5. Wisdom doesn't tell so much as it asks to call forth answers from within
6. There are as many ways of seeing the world as there are people, and all are correct

(because they are correct to the person perceiving)

The bottom line is that a literal reading of this particular story obliterates the possibility of understanding the truths within it. The story itself is wise because it can teach you whatever you see in it – and I've always known God to speak and communicate with me in exactly the right way for me to understand.

God is greater than any literal or superficial description. Every last detail in the *Bible*, for example, doesn't need to be factually true for its message to be accurate or valuable. In this sense I relate very closely to comedian Bill Maher's mocking jokes about the absurdity of believing literally in a "magical man in the sky" who judges and condemns to "everlasting hell" in the name of "love." Yet it also appears that his perception is as limited and dogmatic as the one he mocks.

The reason why I can identify with and relate to both Christians and atheists at the same time is because I see the merits in each perspective. Each also has its limitations. Problems begin to arise when we allow our thinking to become rigid, dogmatic, and exclusionary. Our need to be "right" can overshadow our ability to find common ground and respect other viewpoints. Looking with love makes it possible to expand our perspective and see beyond superficial differences.

You might object that the differences between atheists and, say, fundamentalist Christians are the opposite of superficial. That may be true if the question is, "Does God exist?" However, it may not be if the question is broader, like, "What is the origin and nature of life?"

Answering a question like that can be approached in at least two ways. To simplify, we can say that one approach is through the head and the other is through the heart. An atheist may prefer to emphasize intellect or the head, while a religious fundamentalist may rely primarily on faith, intuition or the heart. This difference is superficial in the sense that in both cases, one mode of understanding is adopted while the other is rejected. Both the atheist and the religious fundamentalist thus perceive only half, at best, of the whole picture. Love, on the other hand, seeks to understand from multiple perspectives and integrates rather than fragments the whole. Dogma says, "either/or". Love says, "both/and".

CAN YOU REALLY CHOOSE HOW TO FEEL ABOUT SOMETHING?

I find this question fascinating. The reason is because it shines a spotlight on an apparent contradiction that has been a kind of recurring theme in my life experiences. The contradiction is this: many masters through the ages have taught that we are the creators of our own life experiences who have the power to control our own responses to whatever situation arises, yet feelings or emotions seem to arise on their own beyond conscious control. The intensity of feelings makes them often the central component of any given experience, so how can it be that we're creating something that seems so out of our control?

This was a major stumbling block for me. And it took a pretty extreme form for me at one point in my life – which I recognize now from a distance as a great gift because it backed me up against a wall and <u>forced</u> me to confront it.

The short version of context is this. In my 20s I started dating a man who was very attractive. He was big, strong, and athletic, and also very open and direct emotionally. He was confident and outgoing so he had a rich social life and lots of friends. We also had a lot in common based on life experiences up to that point, including having lived abroad during most of our adult years. But there was one very significant difference I discovered after we'd been dating for about three months: my default assumption was monogamy and that idea was almost completely absent from his mind, especially as applied to himself.

I know that would be an instant deal-breaker for a lot of people and I had also thought it would be for me. Yet two things made that difficult to follow through with. One was the intensity of my feelings for him. The other was that monogamy as simply a natural expectation in a relationship was something I had never seriously questioned. I just assumed that if the relationship became a serious and committed one then it would be monogamous. Isn't that the way it's supposed to work?

I certainly thought so. And I did everything I could think of to make it work that way. I cried to him about how hurt I felt. I withheld sex when he refused to stop sleeping with someone else. I ignored his claims that it wasn't about me and he didn't want to hurt me, etc. And then when nothing had worked and I was exhausted from the drama of that emotional roller coaster, I issued an ultimatum: choose, or I'll choose for you by leaving for good. By then I meant it. He still resisted.

At crisis points he would give just enough to keep

my hope alive that he might change. Yet he always made it clear that he didn't want to change and that he loved me and felt unfairly pressured to adopt a way of being that felt unnatural to him. He insisted that it was about his male sexual nature and not a reflection on me or my value to him. How can he claim to love me, I wondered, and still do these things that he knows are hurtful to me? There were plenty of echoes there from my past with Mark, the dad I had felt abandoned by. And those painful feelings of worthlessness resurfaced with a vengeance.

At no point in this did I feel in control of my feelings or able even to think I could choose how to feel about it. It would have been absurd to try to feel differently about the situation as I saw it. And I most definitely did not see it as he did.

I took it very personally, as I'm sure most people would. If I were good enough, he wouldn't need anyone else. If I were important enough to him, he would care enough about my feelings to stop hurting them. If only I were…

Though my feelings were very similar, this situation was very different from that with Mark in that there was no epiphany or sudden moment of clarity that shifted my perspective or changed my thoughts and feelings. Yet gradually something did and it became apparent to me only slowly, over time.

It was during this phase of my life that a friend invited me to come to the closing ceremony of an experiential leadership course he had loved. That was my introduction to Lifespring.

Lifespring is a personal growth and leadership

development program similar to the better-known Landmark courses in the U.S. Unlike traditional lecture-based classes, these experiential learning courses operate by putting you in role-play and puzzle-solving types of exercises that push you out of the theoretical into the practical. They require active interaction with the environment and other participants and are designed to get you out of your comfort zone so you can take interpersonal risks in a safe setting.

To me it was both a welcome distraction from my relationship problems and an opportunity to explore new ways of behaving in relation to other people as well as better understand myself. It proved life-changing for me because I jumped in head first and pushed myself to apply what I was learning in my real life. One example: my boyfriend and I had been dating over half a year and neither of us had said "I love you" except maybe once or twice with great awkwardness. The words especially didn't come off my tongue easily and I was extremely reserved about showing affection at all. And the problems we were having sure didn't make it easier!

The Lifespring course required making a commitment to a "stretch" exercise of our choosing to be done outside class over the following week. I resolved to tell him I love him every day for a week. Just the thought of doing it once filled me with anxiety. The idea of making myself so vulnerable terrified me. Yet I was committed to pushing this as far as possible to see what might happen. Would anything change?

That first night, we went to bed and I hadn't done it. So there in the dark I said, "I love you." Several seconds went by in silence, and awkward discomfort was all I felt. Then I heard a soft answer. "That's your problem."

The funny thing is, I couldn't have imagined a response any worse than that, yet I stayed there in the dark next to him and said nothing. There was no trace of cruelty in his tone, and I understood that he was taken off-guard and had no idea how to respond so he just said that. And it didn't kill me. I don't even remember feeling any shame or sense of regret. His answer also caught me off-guard. Hmm… I thought, then slept.

I repeated it the next night. His response was something along the lines of "thank you" and I felt good because it was progress. Saying it the second time was harder than the first, but I'm stubborn and I wasn't about to give up that quickly. After the third night, it started to feel something like a game of "chicken" to me. It was as uncomfortable for him to hear as for me to say, so who would "break" first? I decided it wasn't going to be me!

That exercise had a noticeable effect on both of us. Once he responded by asking "why?" and so I thought about the reasons and told him. In this and other ways, I was changing and he was noticing. He also became softer somehow, more open and curious about these classes he'd dismissed as a waste of time but still couldn't deny the outcomes he was seeing. Then he enrolled.

One other thing found me in that same time period around 1996. That same friend, Steve, who had introduced me to Lifespring, also recommended I read a book called Conversations With God (CWG) by Neale Donald Walsch. I couldn't have felt farther from God than I did then, but the intriguing title and Steve's passionate advocacy of it for me were enough to pique my curiosity so I got my hands on a copy. After reading the first few pages I almost broke down because here, in writing, was the same God I knew as a child. I'd never before encountered anywhere the voice of the God that I had always felt so familiar with. It struck me with an indescribable force. I knew instantly without doubt that it was true and Steve had been right. I was so thankful he had the guts to recommend me something he couldn't possibly have known me well enough to know I needed. So I believed, anyway.

CWG filled in the gaps that Lifespring opened in me. When I read the chapter about the purpose of relationships, it just clicked for me. I saw how I had been looking at mine from a mistaken perspective. I was focusing too much on what I thought I needed and not at all on what I had to offer.

The changes in me that happened at that time were profound and lasting, and now they have some momentum. However, that doesn't mean they just suddenly fixed my relationships. I think it was more like doing the groundwork, preparing the soil. I still had to deal with the issues of my boyfriend's penchant for chasing other women and especially his other "girlfriend" – a long-term relationship with someone he didn't want to marry or live with yet had a child with and still "casually" slept with.

That ultimatum I mentioned earlier, the one I meant and he resisted, was my last resort attempt to resolve a conflict that had stretched into the beginning of the second year of our relationship. The time had come to make good on it so I showed up unexpectedly at his apartment with a bouquet of flowers to say goodbye. I told him that I wanted him to know I loved him but was unable to continue as things are. He was upset about it, and he wasn't alone – his older cousin was in from out of town. I spoke briefly with her, and she already knew about the situation and told me she thought he was acting like an idiot and she knew he loved me, etc. She was very sweet – I hugged her, repeated that I was sad about it but I just couldn't take the emotional drama anymore and didn't know how else to make it stop. My thinking had changed from blaming him to taking responsibility for what I did want.

Several days later he called me, said he'd broken things off with her, and asked if I would see him. I was hesitant, but he persisted so I agreed to a brief meeting outside if he wanted to stop by. (We each had our own apartment although we spent most of our time together. Previously.) We didn't talk long but he seemed different. He assured me it really was over with her, she knew it, and he missed me. Could we give it another try? Maybe we could.

So how do you choose how to feel about something? My answer: you don't because you can't really. How can you feel good about something you think is bad? For me that's just not possible. But guess what you can choose? Your thoughts about something. Every thought you have about something is a story or interpretation about whatever it is relative to you. Your thoughts relate your experience to your sense of self, identity, and self-image. It's like your ego is a sports commentator telling you what just happened and what it means. I look at it like this: if you're going to tell stories in your head about yourself and your life, at least tell stories you like! Put a positive interpretation or spin on it by focusing attention and <u>looking</u> for what to appreciate so <u>you</u> can feel good. Or don't, if you like your negative one better. Just know you're making a choice.

NOTHING BUT LOVE

I woke today a few minutes earlier than usual with this song called "Heartland" by Stick Figure in my mind. Just like the song says in the beginning, the day was beautiful and I was smiling. My heart filled with joy as the chorus replayed in my mind: "nothing but love here, in peace and harmony..." So I got up, made myself a coffee, and went outside in headphones to greet the rainy morning with this uplifting music filling my mind. I was so overcome with love and gratitude that more rain fell from my eyes than the sky. What a wondrous way to start the day!

For years I've heard about the benefits of starting the day with a few minutes of meditation but I actually put it to practice only this year. I've felt pushed for longer than I care to admit to replace some of my bad habits with good ones. Specifically, to give up drinking and smoking for meditation and exercise. Yet I resisted, probably for all the reasons I described in an earlier chapter about the challenges for old dogs learning new tricks.

Now that I've begun the practice of daily meditation, I'm astounded at all it has opened for me. Maybe I shouldn't be, having heard the enthusiastic proclamations of others about how great and powerful a tool it is, but I can attest to the truth that there's a vast difference between knowing something theoretically or intellectually and knowing it experientially. Since beginning the meditation practice, I feel so much more peace, love, joy and gratitude on a regular basis. I easily gave up drinking, which is no small thing for me because I was accustomed to having 1-3 or more glasses of wine daily. I simply realized I was done with it and left it behind like a well-worn teddy bear. And I started writing, heeding another call I'd felt for longer even than the one to stop drinking.

Why did I resist so long doing the things I <u>knew</u> I both needed and even wanted for myself? Put another way, why would I not want to give up things that I knew made me feel bad – which is a different question from asking why not start something new that might prove beneficial (or might not). Thinking about this, I recalled a quote I love that's often misattributed to Nelson Mandela but was actually written by Marianne Williamson in *A Return to Love*. It's worth quoting at length:

> "Our deepest fear is not that we are inadequate. Our deepest fear is that we are powerful beyond measure. It is our light, not our

darkness that most frightens us. We ask ourselves, Who am I to be brilliant, gorgeous, talented, fabulous? Actually, who are you not to be? You are a child of God. Your playing small does not serve the world. There is nothing enlightened about shrinking so that other people won't feel insecure around you. We are all meant to shine, as children do. We were born to make manifest the glory of God that is within us. It is not just in some of us; it is in everyone. And as we let our own light shine, we unconsciously give other people permission to do the same. As we are liberated from our own fear, our presence automatically liberates others."

This idea of being afraid of our own light is a striking one and it resonates deeply for me. Despite a long history of feeling unworthy, a part of me always got its hackles up at that idea and stood firm against it as a kitten can back down a big dog. Sadness and even rage were often present as part of that battle. The true fight of good versus evil, light against darkness, happens within and could never explode outward otherwise. Yet why resist the light or refuse to hear the good news that we are a part of God made manifest in this physical world? Why deny even the possibility that it could be true, that God created you specifically to be able to experience life in physical form through you, through all of us, to know it all at once not just conceptually but experientially? I'm always surprised at how many people who say they believe in God, including attributes of being all-knowing, all-powerful, and in all places at once, somehow still exclude the possibility of God existing within themselves. I can find no logic or sense in this on any level. Yet I think I have an idea about why.

Accepting this idea places an awesome power at your disposal because you can begin to consciously co-create with God. And as we've often heard, with great power comes great responsibility. You simply cannot accept your place in God's Kingdom and still claim ignorance. There is no room left to justify anything with "I didn't know better" or "I couldn't do better because I'm just a powerless human." It's a lot harder to punt when you know that God is excited to go for it and wants to soar with you through those goalposts. Maybe there are just some things we don't want to hear because then we'd have to re-think our whole approach to life.

Another reason why we may rely on religion while holding ourselves apart from our conception of God may be related to a famous observation by Voltaire that "if God did not exist, it would be necessary to invent him." Putting aside the debate about what the author meant, one way of looking at it is that our conception of God represents our ideal. We can call upon perfect power in our powerlessness, and love and healing in our distress. When we feel overwhelmed, we can rely on the immutable and fearless protection and comfort of the greatest ally imaginable. In other words, when we are unable to believe in ourselves we can still turn to an unfailingly reliable source of all that we need.

The thing to be careful about here is that it can be

like a crutch or Oxycontin prescription: it's better than nothing in an extreme situation but can itself be crippling if over-used. Putting your faith in God is great to the extent that it empowers and inspires you to become and be your best self. If that faith turns into an excuse for laziness or apathy, however, or a justification for abdicating personal responsibility to allow God to act through us, then it is not really faith at all. True faith makes you stronger, not weaker. Believing in God is not a "Get Out of Hell Free" card – it's more like a summons to stand up and live as a witness testifying to your faith through the quality of your being, in practice, at all times. Just as a tree is known by its fruit, so, too, are we. Faith overcomes fear, and a true believer in the glory of God strives to recognize and nurture the Divine spark within to bring it alive in the world of form. The power and love of Jesus, for example, derive from a complete acceptance, not rejection, of his oneness with God. We are called to seek and see the same in ourselves. "Imitation is the sincerest form of flattery" means that we seek to emulate those we truly respect and most admire. Anything less is just lip service. This is why true faith inspires us to lift ourselves up as high as possible to be our best selves. There is no truer form of worship than to become like our ideal.

♥

THOUGHTS ARE MARINADE FOR THE MIND

How would you describe the inner world of your mind? Is it calm and peaceful, with thoughts floating by that you pluck, consider and then choose whether to hold onto or release? Is it more like a rushing vortex of thoughts circling chaotically with some having hooks that attach onto you easily but are difficult to release? What does it feel like in there?

If you've ever stepped back in awareness to attempt a simple observation of your own mind, you might have noticed that you are not your thoughts (otherwise, how could you observe them?), and the act of consciously observing them tends to slow them down. This is the essence of meditation. Normally we're so caught up in chasing and following thoughts that we can fail to recognize that moment of choice determining which thoughts carry us along while others go along without catching our attention. In other words, thoughts of all kinds are always flowing through the field of our awareness, but some seem to be stickier than others. Some attach to you like a magnet to a refrigerator door and others just brush the surface and fall off. What kinds of thoughts are the stickiest for you?

For me, it's usually the ones that have the strongest emotional resonance in the moment. So after an argument with a family member, for example, I notice a lot of thoughts related to the topic of the argument, replays of things that were actually said, clever rejoinders I wish I'd thought of at the time, memories of past arguments, and so on. There might also be others, like the appearance of a hummingbird or something connected to a research project I've been working on, but they don't stick. The ones that stick most easily are those that match up with what I'm already feeling, and magnify it.

If I do nothing to interfere with this process, soon my mind is filled completely with thoughts about the argument in almost every possible configuration and extension of those particular ideas. This massing of thoughts about the argument fuels the emotional reaction and strengthens it, too. Even well after the argument has ended, I'm experiencing an extended and usually even more intense version of it inside my own head. Now the thoughts and emotions are all twisted together in a huge ball of "black funk" that has completely taken over my mind. It can take hours or even longer to unwind.

It is these kinds of thoughts – the ones imbued with significant emotional energy – that are the most powerful creators of my mental state. They're also the ones that will most strongly influence how (or even whether) I talk to the people around me, what words I choose and tone I use. They also determine to a large degree what I do physically – if I go for a drive in that state, for example, I'm much more likely to drive aggressively and swear at other drivers (perhaps even loud enough for them to hear). What I won't do is sit still so the cat can come sleep on my lap. Or sing a joyful song with my daughter. Because those things just don't match the thoughts and emotions I'm currently holding.

Now the question is, if this is a familiar pattern for me then how do I break it? How can I focus on love instead of fear or frustration?

The one thing that changes everything is awareness. This might be easiest to see with the help of an example. If you've parented or even babysat a toddler, you probably learned pretty quickly how to recognize the signs of an impending meltdown. If your two-year-old is tired and over-stimulated, maybe the little one gets extra whiney or takes toys aggressively from another child. When you see that behavior, you realize that your little angel will bite the other child in a few minutes if you don't separate them, because you've seen it happen before. You know the pattern and you are aware of the warning signs. You can act to intervene before the whole scenario plays out.

Having this level of awareness is easier for most of us when we're observing others than when we ourselves are caught up in a situation. Yet it can be cultivated even then. I've found it helpful to stop long enough to take one deep breath and ask myself,

"What's going on here?" The question serves to lift my perspective as if I am rising up five feet in the air to see with a little detachment. "Oh, I'm being attacked verbally. Usually I try to defend myself and attack back and then a barrage of shouting begins." Just that moment of awareness at a slightly higher level gives me some space to consider a different response. If I don't know what to do, just that I don't want to repeat that familiar pattern because it always ends with me feeling upset, usually I don't do anything. This itself is different enough – I just stay quiet, look and listen so the angry person doesn't feel provoked by being ignored, but keeping my thoughts to myself. No argument ensues because it takes two to argue and I took a "time out" to avoid escalation. When things calm down, I can return to the issue and share whatever I need to, and by then I will have had time to filter and refine my thoughts and also temper my emotions.

In this I see an improvement from an all-out argument. It still leaves me unsatisfied because I'm absorbing someone else's negative tirade, which I'd prefer to avoid. So I start thinking about how I could respond to defuse it faster or even stop it as soon as it starts. Now I can play out that scenario in my mind, where I respond calmly and lovingly to preserve my own peace of mind. The more I think this way, the easier it gets for me to try it out whenever the next conflict arises. But I'm focusing not on the conflict – I'm focusing on myself feeling peaceful and calmly becoming aware of my surroundings. I see myself staying above the fray, so to speak. I practice this with the little things because they're easier and more frequent. The more I practice, the less irritated I get when a new conflict arises. A calmer mood makes me less likely to descend into a downward spiral of negative emotion.

This also works if I'm the grouchy one, the cause of the drama. All it takes is a moment of checking in with myself to see how I'm feeling to bring the emotion into conscious awareness. I might easily identify the cause – like being hungry or not sleeping well last night or in pain from an injury – but if not I don't waste mental energy on it. I save that energy so I can consciously redirect my focus toward a more peaceful feeling, maybe just by closing my eyes, breathing deeply, and calling to mind something that makes me smile. I might simply focus on my desire to feel better.

This is a meditative practice in consciously cultivating a desired direction of thinking. It's about selectively choosing to hold thoughts that are consistent with the desired direction and releasing those that aren't. It takes some vigilance if it's an effort to overcome a bad mood. Usually it's most helpful to focus first on letting go of negative thoughts. Vigilance means noticing what kinds of thoughts are occupying my attention and telling myself it's time to move on, I'm done with this thought, my desire right now is peace, and so on. Sometimes just repeating that intention enough times will crowd out everything else until a new, more pleasant thought comes along to hold onto. There are many rafts in the sea of thoughts and the goal is to choose with conscious intention which to grab onto.

Just as a marinade will infuse a piece of meat that

sits in it long enough, the thoughts we hold onto long enough infuse our minds. It has a cumulative effect over time, which is why choosing your thoughts consciously is so important. If you marinade a steak in sour milk, it will taste awful no matter how good the cut of beef may be. You don't just throw a rib eye in a bag with random liquids for hours and expect it to taste good! The more expensive the steak, the more you care about the quality of ingredients in your marinade, right? So what do you choose to marinade the filet mignon of your mind in?

When your marinade is made up of ingredients that reflect your desires, your mind gets saturated with the images and feelings associated with the desire. If your thoughts are "I can't afford it" or "I'm not _____ enough to do it successfully" then your sour milk marinade will spoil your feast. If your thoughts are "the sand feels so good between my toes" or "seeing my book on the New York Times Bestseller List would be such a thrill" then your motivation will increase to do what you can to make it happen. This marinade prepares you to act on opportunities.

The first time I experienced this working powerfully for me in service of my conscious desire was when I was in college. Reading through the course book in the summer before my first year, I had discovered a major in international relations and it immediately showed itself as my path. It combined everything I was interested in without requiring me to choose among its major disciplines of history, language study and literature, economics, and government with a focus on foreign policy. This was 1988 and I was familiar with

President Reagan's characterization of the Soviet Union as an "Evil Empire" that posed an existential threat to the world with its nuclear weapons. I'm naturally disinclined to just take someone's word for something so I wanted to learn and decide for myself what to think about it. I pursued the major and began learning Russian so that I could truly and deeply understand this other Super Power and how the Russians think. Sting's song, "The Russians," resonated strongly with me.

My major required at least a semester abroad, and junior year was the time when most students studied abroad. To take that semester in the Soviet Union, however, required three full years of college-level language classes just to apply so to be eligible I would have to take the full third year in an intensive summer course after my second year. I did that and then applied for a program in Moscow for the spring semester of junior year.

In early February 1991 I went to Moscow. Aside from a few trips to Tijuana and one into Victoria, British Columbia, Canada, I'd never been outside the U.S. Yet there I was, halfway around the world in "the land of the enemy" learning the Russian language, culture, and literature. No one else in my family even had a passport and they jokingly called me "Commie" (as opposed to "Kimmie" as I'd been called when I was younger).

During the spring of 1991, change was in the air in Moscow. Gorbachev's policy of "glasnost" had been introduced a few years earlier and momentum was building toward greater openness with the West. Boris

Yeltsin was beginning to make a name for himself and, for the first time, there was a public referendum on price liberalization. This was a big deal because those kinds of decisions were normally tightly controlled and the opinions of ordinary people weren't usually sought. But that was changing, and there was a sense of electric expectation in Moscow that I found fascinating. I wondered what the future held and what kinds of other changes might be on the horizon.

After about the third month of my planned four-month stay, which had included three weeks living with the family of one of the institute's female students, I felt like I was just getting on my feet with the language and wished I didn't have to leave so soon. My studies had concentrated on the Cold War between the US and USSR, and living in the capital of the Soviet Union was an intoxicating learning experience. Leaving when things were just getting interesting was deeply disappointing. The more I thought about it, the more I wanted to stay.

But how? I still had a year of college left. I had a student visa that was expiring at the end of the semester and a group flight back to the US. The only option I saw was to follow through with that.

But... But... Still I wanted to be in Moscow, not back in California. Maybe I could go home with the group, and then come back. Maybe I could take a year off school. If I worked all summer, maybe I could earn enough to buy a plane ticket. If I asked the family I stayed with, maybe I could get an invitation to obtain a private tourist visa. Maybe I could...

My desire to be in Moscow was all I could think

about during that last month. Making international calls at that time in Moscow required a burdensome process of submitting a request in writing at the central post office and waiting in line for hours to access a phone that allowed such calls. I went and stood in the freezing February cold to make two calls – one to my college to see if I could get an academic deferral for a year because I had no idea if it was even possible. The other was to my parents to let them know how I was doing and gauge their reaction to the possibility that I might want to come back after this semester was over. The college said yes, I could defer my last year and that wouldn't change my financial aid arrangements. As for parents, the idea came as a shock and did not exactly spark an enthusiastic response.

With no plan in place or even any real idea how to make it happen, knowing only that I wanted to come back more than I could remember ever wanting anything, I packed for the flight home. None of my warm winter clothes made it into that suitcase. The beautiful London Fog coat my grandparents had splurged to buy me for the trip stayed behind with my Russian family, too. I wouldn't need those things in California anyway, but I wasn't giving them away because I had every intention of using them again.

My dad asked on the way home from the airport why I had so much less luggage than when I left. I told him it was because I'd left my winter clothes there. He observed that I'd said on the phone I was thinking about going back and he didn't realize that meant I'd already decided to. I hadn't, either – yet now it's clear to me that although I denied it at the time I actually had on some level already made the decision. I thought so much about my desire that everything I did supported it even without a conscious decision to do it.

I worked all summer in a liquor store because it paid well enough to buy a round trip ticket to Europe with an open-ended return date during a one-year period. It was a Boston-Berlin route. I had a 30-day single-entry tourist visa. I had a good friend, Jill, from college who had just graduated, lived in Boston, and would take the same flight with me to Berlin and then we'd take the train together to Moscow. I had a couple hundred dollars for food and living expenses. I had my dream.

Here is what I did NOT have: a place to stay beyond the first couple days, a job, enough money to last more than a few weeks, or any idea how to get a longer-term visa. I had no plan for how to solve any of these problems, either. I figured I would work it out when I got there.

I was going on a wing and a prayer.

In the weeks prior to my intended departure in September, I was completely immersed in my desire to go and simply ignored all thoughts about why it wouldn't work. My family's insistence that I was nuts, my dad's deep concern that I was throwing away my education (and his investment), and all the uncertainty about how things would turn out were tuned out. I dismissed them all because the desire to go was so strong nothing could deflect me from its path. I was all in.

Toward the end of August, President Gorbachev was held under house arrest in Crimea as a hardline coup attempted to oust him from power. This, of all things, came closest to derailing my plans. Images of Boris Yeltsin on a tank in central Moscow flooded the airwaves and my parents and relatives strongly urged me to cancel the trip. Yet all I could think was, "This happens now, when I'm not there?!" The Soviet Union was disintegrating and I was missing it! This was history! How I thought about it made me want to go more, not less.

In September, I did go. Within 48 hours of arrival I had a job that provided a one-year work visa and paid well enough to rent an apartment. I made some of the best friends of my life and stayed almost a full year that included a three-month stint in Yekaterinburg, Boris Yeltsin's hometown in the heart of Russia at the base of the Urals mountain range on the border of Europe and Asia. I fell in love, not just with the country and its culture but also with a man who followed me back to California when it came time to leave in the summer. I finished my last year at Pomona College and then, out of the blue, got a job offer back in Moscow. I chose that over enrolling in law school and, though it led down the line to the end of my relationship, I returned to the land of my dreams with degree in hand and confidence coming from experience that all would be well.

Had I zeroed in on all the reasons why it made no sense and couldn't work, I never would have even attempted to follow that dream. I had to believe in it for it to be possible. I had to desire it so strongly that I didn't care about the obstacles enough to even look at them. Failure was a possibility beyond consideration and I refused to even entertain it as an option. It was almost like I was possessed – I had been marinating so completely in my thoughts of "this must happen" for so long that my focus on achieving it became single-minded and laser-like. Somehow everything I needed came to me and I just had to be open and willing to say yes. The ground was already prepared by my single-minded focus on what I loved.

♥

GOD, I LOVE THIS GOOD EARTH!

I first realized how much I love our planet a few years ago. Before then I had never really given it much thought. Seeing pictures of Earth from space was pretty cool and there are certainly places I've been where the natural beauty took my breath away, but I didn't feel any emotional connection to the planet as a whole. Perhaps that began to change when I started hearing about climate change and seeing images of the incredible destruction we humans have wrought. Oil spills that tarred marine birds black, smoke billowing into an already dead-looking sky, unimaginably huge piles of plastic waste and the like were such a viscerally disturbing departure from the pristine beauty I took for granted. Fear overtook me that we were killing this planet and sadness hit like a ton of sludge. I cried.

Later I realized that the planet would survive, as it has already been through far more tumultuous times in its multi-billion year history. We humans might not survive, but Earth would. My relief at that was tempered by the anger I felt at how we humans were impacting our planet like cancer attacks our bodies. That anger said we all deserve to die and I felt solidarity, one with the Earth and not the human race. What an odd and awkward place to be.

I don't wish for humanity's demise. I wish for our awakening. I wish for us to see with the eyes of love so we stop the unnecessary destruction and become the guardians and stewards of the world that we are capable of being. I want us to look with awe and appreciation at the beauty of creation – the natural world and our own contributions to our environment.

As a fish has no concept of water until it's out of it, I think people also take very much for granted our environment. This applies not only to our lovely blue and green planet, of course, but also to the more immediate aspects of our surroundings. At the risk of taking the metaphor too far: if thoughts are marinade, then our environment is the stew.

That we are deeply influenced by what surrounds us is so obvious it's easy to miss. It's not quite like a chameleon changing colors within minutes but it's not all that different, either. It just happens more subtly than suddenly. And like the chameleon, we're rarely aware of it as it's happening. It's the kind of thing you might not notice until you leave a familiar place to live for a while elsewhere. Obviously going abroad highlights this but so does going away for college or relocating to another state (perhaps even city) for work.

With the advent of cable and the Internet, we now

also share a large and growing "virtual" environment with many voices clamoring for attention. As previously mentioned, media tends to highlight problems and hype anything that will draw a crowd. For this reason, it plays a significant role in fomenting contention and conflict, particularly where politics in this country is concerned. The political climate has become so hostile in recent decades that candidates on both sides of the aisle are routinely demonized by the other side and compromise has come to be seen as weakness. In an environment of such bitter conflict, how could peace possibly prevail?

That is not the kind of stew I want to be in! It reminds me too much of mixing milk with lemon juice. I realized that when I watch the news, read articles, browse social media, flip channels on TV and so on, I start to look at this country as a bunch of greedy, selfish, whining cowards who have exactly the awful government they deserve. Not very loving! Yet when I look at my personal life, family, friends, neighbors and co-workers, I see people who are caring, funny, kind, and generous. I love my life! Two very different environments lead to two vastly different feelings about people. And I don't even have to leave this place to see that.

I doubt I'm alone in being this sensitive to the mood around me. Emotions feel like static electricity that passes easily from one person to another. I like feeling good, not bad, happy instead of angry. I've said a lot about how crucial thoughts are in determining emotional reactions, but much less about the role of environment.

We seem to know instinctively that a toxic environment is bad for us, whether the poisons are physical and chemical or emotional. Being around people who are critical, angry, pessimistic and otherwise negative is a surefire way to drain our energy and bring us down. If someone smiles at you, on the other hand, or greets you enthusiastically, then you'll probably smile back and feel your mood lift. Even if you're having a bad day, an unexpected act of kindness can turn it around. Yet how often do we consciously choose to shape our environment so that it uplifts us and supports the emotional state we want for ourselves? And how often do we just go along with what's easy and familiar?

Stop for just a moment and look around where you are. Do the things you see bring a smile of appreciation to your face? Do you enjoy being where you are? Does it feel safe, comfortable, and beautiful? Or, perhaps, are you retreating into a book because you don't really like where you are? Is there a lot of clutter or other things there that remind you of a thousand unfinished tasks on your to-do list? Does your everyday space calm you or overwhelm you? And what might it feel like if you arranged your space specifically to soothe you, remind you of what you love, and encourage you to pursue your freedom to grow and play? If you look at your favorite music and television programs, does watching and listening to them inspire the best in you? Do they make you feel good about other people and your life in general? And if not, why? Why did you choose them?

This is an area of my life that I didn't give much

attention to until recently. Except in extreme cases, perhaps, like when I used to listen to political talk radio and decided to quit because some of the show hosts would say outrageous things that, well, outraged me. But a couple months ago as I was walking through a store a small book caught my eye. Its well-chosen title compelled me to pick it up: *The Life-Changing Magic of Tidying Up* by Marie Kondo. So I bought it because it had a clear process for putting things in order and I'd been growing increasingly annoyed with the mounting pile of clutter in my office. Although "life-changing" seemed overblown, I liked the author's approach and decided to give it a go.

As recommended, I started with my clothes (all of which are in a single closet split between hangers and drawers). Using the method described in that book, I sorted everything and discarded half of what I had, giving the one half to Goodwill and organizing the other as advised. I was shocked to discover that I started to actually enjoy opening my closet door and choosing what to wear! I should note that I hate shopping and don't care much about clothes so you can appreciate what a change this was for me. Getting to my office, however, was daunting so I didn't right away. After a few weeks of noticing my appreciation for my closet every day, the desire to similarly transform my office grew and grew.

Once I started, my office was done within about two weeks. The difference was phenomenal! It went from being a cluttered mess I hated to look at to becoming an open, inviting space I love to work and relax in. I purposely left empty an entire shelf and a couple walls so I could see and feel expansive space around. The funny thing is, the author was right. It really has proven life-changing! I feel calmer, more peaceful, more in control of my life, and happy to have room to grow as a person. My space now supports my forward movement, optimism, and overall happiness.

I got so inspired that last week I took the same approach to my DVR. I deleted all but maybe 10% of recorded shows and series set to record automatically. I left only those that make me laugh without unduly reinforcing negative stereotypes or encouraging anything I don't want in my life (for example, no crime detective shows). And I haven't been on Netflix since. I stopped looking at Facebook a couple months ago, too. All of this has made me happier and more productive.

I'm sure eventually I'll get back to Netflix, for example, and maybe look at Facebook once a month or so. When I do, you can be sure I will be choosing carefully. For example, Netflix has a lot of great TED talks, comedy, etc., that I'll turn to for entertainment. Yes, it does take effort to be my own curator, and finding content that aligns with my desired quality of life is more challenging than I'd like, but I'm convinced it's worth the effort. "Garbage in, garbage out" applies to everything, really. That's not what I want for my life.

What I want for my life is love and happiness, beauty and joy. Looking at the wisteria blooms outside my window, with buzzing bees in the sunlight after almost two weeks of very needed rain, I know I have it all if I choose to see it. I don't miss Facebook or "Scandal" or wine or clutter or political drama. I welcome light, laughter, love, friendship, good health, and fun.

Pulling my thoughts and environment into intentional alignment with my desires has already proven much more beneficial for me than I could have imagined when I started. The irony is that I didn't plan to make all these changes at first – but making one led to the next, then the next, and the next after that. I'm so grateful!

Looking beyond my own personal space, I see myself surrounded by glorious beauty. Our yard is a colorful and bountiful sanctuary that was co-created by God and my husband. He is an artist who loves to select and plant new life, whether in his work or more literally in the ground outside. Aside from the wisteria I mentioned before, there are fruit trees, a vegetable garden, jasmine just now blooming, and many shrubs and flowers that attract bees, butterflies and hummingbirds. Looking out on it reminds me of the beauty of life and the magic of nature that renews itself each spring. It feels like the Garden of Eden is here, now. Starting the day by stepping outside, especially as the sun is coming up, fills me with hope and anticipation.

Recently I was talking via text messages with my sister and aunt, with whom my sister and I have had a particularly loving bond since we were small. There was a short period of about six months when I was in second grade and sis was in kindergarten that was challenging for our mom so her older sister and her husband offered to have us live with them temporarily. During that time our aunt and uncle, who are practicing Catholics, put my sister and me in private Catholic schools and gave us a record called "Hi God" as a gift. It was actually two LPs of acoustic music celebrating God and life that my sister and I both loved and listened to constantly. We used to love putting on our own shows, particularly for our grandparents who showered us with appreciation for it, so we knew all the words to all the songs. We were reminiscing about this in our text messages, and our aunt later e-mailed me a link: she had found a recording on CD of that album on Amazon! I was stunned because it never occurred to me that a fairly obscure recording from 40 years ago could be there! But it was, and I ordered it.

Listening to it all these years later brought such a sense of joy and wonder! The message resonates as much as it ever did and brings me back to that place of childhood openness and glee. My 13-year-old daughter certainly laughed to see me dancing around to it and, though I may have felt a bit silly, I couldn't stop smiling, singing, and dancing. It felt so liberating to put aside my seriousness to embrace a childlike playfulness and I realized how much I'd like to have more of that in my life. Being an adult seems so conceptually intertwined with seriousness, it got me thinking about how and why that happens.

When my daughter was a toddler she was an exuberant bundle of energy. She had an adorable crinkly-nosed grin and wide-eyed curiosity about absolutely everything. She had barely learned to walk and loved wearing my knee-high boots to prance around (on her, of course, they went all the way up to her hips!). The first time she got into my closet, found and put them on, my initial thought was, she needs to stay out of my closet. But as I looked at her with pure joy on her face, that thought just melted in my laughter. She was having so much fun it infected me instantly.

I was raised in the shadow of a "children should be seen and not heard" mentality that expects children to conform to adult expectations. It was, play quietly or go outside if you want to make noise. Be quiet in the car. Be quiet and sit still at the dinner table. Don't interrupt adults when they're talking. And so on.

I imagine this is familiar to many of you. You probably also experienced this stifling atmosphere as a child because it was a very widespread parenting practice. When I became a parent myself, these were the expectations I carried from my own experience. Yet I had seen a few examples of people doing it differently. One that stuck out for me was before our daughter was born, when my husband and I had traveled to Vancouver to visit some friends we hadn't seen in years. The couple had a little girl who was maybe 18 months old. We met for lunch at a café on the waterfront.

Not long into it, before the food came, their daughter was getting restless and wanted to get out of her high chair. There were no other patrons in the room and our friends let her down. She started, unsurprisingly, to wander all over the room, making lots of happy noise. We four adults were also trying to carry on a conversation. And then my friend surprised me: she excused herself and went to follow her daughter, letting her outside to follow the ducks and explore.

My reaction was one of surprise and, I'll admit, some irritation because we'd traveled a long way to see them and here she was letting a toddler outside to explore rather than talking to us. In my family, the child would be left in the high chair and expected to sit still for the meal and accommodate the adults. And it occurred to me that my friend's behavior actually made a lot more sense. Why should a two-year-old be expected to understand and accommodate better than a thirty-something adult?! Why do so few adults see a child's curiosity as endearing and fun instead of as a nuisance? Why should my comfort as an adult take precedence over the wonderment of a child and especially the child's capability to manage her emotions of restlessness or boredom? I've had years to practice that skill! Realizing that shifted my perception of my friend's choices 180 degrees.

When my own daughter was the toddler in a restaurant, especially when we were there with members from my family, I began to understand the intense pressure our society puts on parents to "control your children!" My daughter's curiosity was a burden to other people and I felt judged negatively as a mother for expecting less from my toddler in terms of self-control than from my adult family members in terms of understanding. Often I could tell that they didn't want to be around her. She definitely felt it, too.

The way I looked at it was, as she grows she'll learn to take other people's preferences and boundaries into consideration. Her self-control will get better. Most importantly, I could guide her but it would be to her benefit to learn for herself that boundaries vary by person and she needs to ask rather than assume.

I know some family members felt uncomfortable with

my approach, at least in part because they didn't want to feel responsible for watching my child all the time. I didn't have the option of limiting these interactions to my own home because my relatives so rarely visit us – they live pretty near to each other while we live farther away, and so most often it's us doing the traveling. Not easy with a small child, but it was that or no visits at all so we'd go. My "unruly" – by their standards – child would be loose in their homes. That inevitably meant her getting into things she shouldn't and sometimes breaking things.

This was a horrible position for me as her mother to be in. Of course, I spent time teaching her to respect other people's things, ask first, etc. But I chose not to physically confine her or follow her around constantly even when she was a toddler. I had a strong philosophical reason for that. The only way to keep her from ever "trespassing" beyond someone else's boundaries would be for me to set her boundaries closer and tighter than anyone else would – put her on a short leash, so to speak. Otherwise, she might not cross one person's but she would another's. What would be the cost to her of being on that short leash? Sure, she wouldn't step on any toes. But she'd be like that elephant tied with a rope to a pole and just learn to hold herself back, never even trying for what she wants because she'd be so used to hearing, "no." I feared this more than my family's disapproval. If I didn't set that boundary, then she would find them for herself and learn to try, not pull back in fear. Maybe she would end up with fewer self-imposed limitations on herself. Maybe she would learn things like respect, sensitivity, and persuasiveness from having to navigate these waters herself.

Looking at her now, I don't regret that choice. In fact, I wonder how it would be if we encouraged more actively curiosity and exploration in children, and adults too. This doesn't mean there are no boundaries or it's OK to just do what you want without a care for anyone else. But it does mean, don't be afraid to try. It also means that we would all need to learn how to set boundaries with others in a way that is gentle, yet firm. This is what will teach respect for boundaries. We need to be willing to accept and live with some discomfort and inconvenience. Yet it can also open new opportunities. For example, a lot more places could be designed to be "explorer-friendly." Others can be adults-only. But curiosity and exploration can be encouraged much more broadly, if we let go of some of our "look but don't touch" mentality toward life. Some private companies, like Google and Facebook, are known for building fun into their environments but this approach could spread a lot more into the public realm. Interactive museums are a great improvement over roped-off exhibits, and there are a lot more places where our culture could give us more freedom to play and have fun.

"No" is one of the first words we learn, and teach our children. What if we said "Yes!" instead? Yes to crazy clothes and hair, even at work. Yes to creative self-expression in any way that doesn't harm others. Yes to playfulness, pushing boundaries, and personalizing our possessions like the art cars and costumes of Burning Man. Yes to fun, yes to beauty, yes to life!

Did you ever stop to wonder whether all your judgments about the way things "should" be are crowding out your youthful wonder and willingness to appreciate and even celebrate what is already wonderful? What might you do just for fun if you had no worries about not being taken seriously or being judged as silly? How wonderful would the world seem if you looked to find and bring joy? Maybe you don't feel comfortable dyeing your hair purple, but could you smile at seeing someone else's purple hair? When you see something you would normally judge and reject as inappropriate, as long as it's not hurting anybody try to change your filter from "adult eyes" to "child's curiosity" and look closer. Can you find in it anything to appreciate, enjoy, or admire? And if not, can you just shrug and let it go? Some people's fashion choices just make me shake my head in bafflement, like teenage guys wearing their pants below their hips and even their butts, for example. Although it's not my favorite look and I would never wear it, I just laugh to myself when I see it and wonder what holds the pants up or how they can walk that way. It's not for me but I can accept it for them. It's one of many threads in the beautiful tapestry of this world I love.

LOVE MORE

I was in high school when I experienced for the first time an immediate and powerful response to a prayer. Although the details escape my recollection, I remember very well how I was feeling: despondent. I felt very disconnected from everyone around me. In addition to having essentially no relationship with my father, Mark, or my sister, the relationships I had with the few school friends I had and my mom and dad were rather superficial. I didn't share much with anyone about what was really going on inside me and felt like there was a gaping hole in my soul.

I know, looking back, that my parents loved me but at the time I didn't feel that. It seemed they had no interest in anything I was involved with, from sports to music to academics. They saw me as argumentative when, to me, debate was simply curiosity and intellectual challenge. As a child I asked a lot of questions, always wanting to know how something worked or why things were as they were, and often I would find inconsistencies or holes in an explanation so would challenge what I was told. I simply couldn't accept an answer at face value and would dig deeper, looking to see whatever it was from a different point of view. I can see how this could be exhausting for my parents but I never felt I was arguing for the sake of argument. I wanted to explore and understand things deeply and debate was a great way to do that. Neither my mom or dad was really interested in engaging in these kinds of conversations, however, and they would often end them by saying something like, "If I said it's black, you'd argue it's white so there's no point talking about it." I doubt they intended it but the message I got was, "You don't know what you're talking about and your opinions don't matter." So I kept a lot to myself.

Feeling lonely and misunderstood, I just lay on my bed sobbing. I didn't feel close to anyone and couldn't see any point to life in general. As my sobbing shook my whole body, I cried out in my mind for help. "Please help me" repeated until suddenly I felt an overwhelming sense of peace wash over me. My body went still, the crying stopped, and my mind seemed to just let go and float away. It was unexpected and blissful. I immediately started praying in gratitude. Feeling that presence of peace within me, I reflected on my impression that there wasn't enough love in my life. I asked, please, tell me, how can I have more love in my life? I desperately wanted to know.

I got an answer that stunned me to my core. I heard the two words so clearly it was as if they were spoken aloud into my ears. That itself shocked me because I'd never felt or heard an answer to a prayer like that before, but this was unmistakable and I knew it couldn't have come from me. There was just no way I could have come up with that answer on my own. The two words were, "Love more."

Those two little words flipped everything upside down and profoundly challenged what I thought I knew. It was so simple, elegant, and clear that it opened my mind in a completely new way. The answer implied that what I desired was within me to have and give, and under my control, not outside or dependent on others. It was a powerful connecting point later when I read CWG, which also advocated that the fastest way to get what we seek for ourselves is to give it to others because you can only give what you already have.

There was one other time in my life, maybe 15 years later, when I got a similarly clear and surprising answer to a heartfelt prayer. I was feeling frustrated with life and its challenges, particularly my close relationships and also a more general sense of how messed up the world seemed to me. I felt a strong longing for God, like I was not where I belonged and wanted to go "home" almost badly enough to end my life but afraid to do so. My prayer was essentially, "I don't want to be here anymore; I want to be with You." It wasn't the case that my life was particularly bad, but more that it still seemed unfulfilled. I wanted to be with God.

The answer that came was, "You don't have to leave your body for that to happen." I was amazed at the possibility existing that I could be with God while still in this life. It made perfect sense to me, and even seemed ridiculous that I hadn't realized it before. I recalled the times when I've felt close to God and how transcendent some of those experiences were. Maybe I could have more of them... It's a very "in the moment" feeling but the effect is powerful and lasting, unforgettable even.

"Love more." "You don't have to leave your body to be with God." These moments, and others that were no less inspired, though different in being more visual than verbal, have exerted a profound influence on me. They felt and continue to feel sacred. They were deeply moving, emotionally intense, and mind-expanding insights that fundamentally shifted my thinking. They opened my eyes and mind to the fact that things can be very different from how they might seem on the outside. Subtle shifts can have a profound impact. Yet such insights have only ever come to me when I was open and seeking answers rather than believing or assuming I already knew. With only one (relatively recent) exception, I have never been struck by a powerful spiritual truth without having first asked a question – one born from intense emotion and extremely potent desperation to know, with equally strong willingness to receive an answer and accept the unexpected. Nor can I think of a single time when these elements have all come together in me that I failed to receive the guidance I sought. Never have I ever felt misled, either.

I don't think this is relevant only to people who believe in God. Another way to look at it would be that intuition and creative insights are available to all of us, regardless of whether or not we believe in God. Inspiration isn't only for the religious. Curiosity, deep

THIS LOVE IS FOR YOU

thinking, and full focus on an issue have led to countless breakthroughs and innovations that the inspired individuals may not attribute to God but words are separate from substance. Energy and creativity hardly care what you call them. What's important is that openness to a new way of looking at things is essential for growth and learning. When I thought there wasn't enough love in my life, what I needed wasn't for all the people around me to change, but for me to be willing to change the way I looked at things. I needed to look within myself to see a way out of what was causing me pain. I needed to be willing to change myself. *"Love more" meant that my own love would increase the love in my life, and also that my own love would attract more love in response.* That's a powerful combination – one that cannot fail when applied and acted upon. "The only things we ever keep are those we give away."[6]

---

[6] "Love That Is Kept Inside" from *Hi God!* by Carey Landry & Carol Jean Kinghorn

♥

WOULD YOU... MIND?

The single most powerful tool at your disposal is one you've probably never learned – or been taught – how to use. By the time you're reading this, you've likely had thousands of hours practicing how to follow directions given by others, starting well before school began and continuing to this day. But where and when have you been taught how your brain works, what your mind is capable of, or how to use that effectively for your own benefit?

If you were educated in the American public school system, as I was, then the vast majority of your "education" revolved around following a prescribed routine, sitting still for hours on end, and listening to other people tell you what to do and how to do it. If you complied, you were rewarded with gold stars and then little letters on a piece of paper telling you how "smart" or "successful" you were at pleasing others (primarily your teacher and parents). If not, you were considered a troublemaker, deprived of the little freedom you had, and labeled in some negative way ("disruptive" or "slow learner" or whatever other creative attribution those dissatisfied others could come up with).

Since we humans have such a strong tendency to fear and avoid change, our public education system still operates on the principles and in service of the goals that were important at the time of its creation a century ago. Industry was just ascending then, and Henry Ford's ingenious conveyor belt adoption for factory-based manufacturing was dramatically changing American business. These new factories needed workers, and the skills they demanded were quite different from what most people had learned. In particular, the production system relied upon specialization of tasks – done by both machine and human working together – and rapid repetition. This is great for efficiency because once you learn how to do the one thing required of you, repetition allows you to repeat it accurately and quickly so you can do more and more work in less and less time. It's horrible for the human soul, however, because the mind-dulling monotony will bore you to death and possibly even cause physical injury or death if lack of focus causes a careless mistake that gets you caught in the machinery. The connection to schools, of course, is that they were designed as training grounds for the next generation of factory workers. High on the list of priorities for instruction was skill development in the areas of patience, following directions, and keeping with the pace of the entire group. What was low on the list? Autonomous thinking.

Most of those jobs have left America but our education system still trains us for them. What it fails to train us for is living an independent life as an individual and as a cooperative team player. And since thinking for yourself is actually a disadvantage for an assembly-line worker, nothing in the education system could prepare you adequately for that. Even if you were privileged enough to go to private school, most likely your experience was substantially similar because most private schools still follow the same basic model. That includes regimented start and end times, other-directed learning (meaning someone other than the student chooses the topics, their order, and what is included and excluded from each), and so on.

It's also likely that your family followed the same model, for several reasons. One is that the structure of an enterprise matched up with traditional family structures in which one person (the father, usually) is in charge and everyone else defers to his leadership. This basic structure permeates all of our social systems, from companies to families and religion to politics. Another aspect is that parents rarely tend to teach and encourage their children to think for themselves or question authority because that might undermine their authority!

For all these reasons, if you have learned to think for yourself, very likely you are self-taught. Some people might be offended at the suggestion that they don't think for themselves, and that's certainly understandable. Paradoxically somewhat, our culture still reveres rugged individualism, at least in popular culture – like movies – if not real life. My intention is simply to point out the many factors acting "under the radar" to discourage all of us from thinking for ourselves.

The last couple decades have brought unprecedented discoveries about the human brain, psychology, and cognition. Little to none of that has made its way into education. It has, however, been put to powerful use in private enterprise, particularly in marketing and advertising. What this means, unfortunately, is that ordinary individuals are subject to potent manipulation without being aware of it. How to motivate people to do or avoid doing something is an entire field of inquiry that few of us know anything about. We've all heard of reverse psychology so we can recognize when someone uses it on us, and that recognition is a form of protection against that manipulation. What protection do you have against forms of manipulation that you are unable to recognize for what they are?

The upshot from all of this boils down to this foundational idea: the mind most definitely can be trained, and your mind has been and continues to be trained – but not by you, mostly, and not necessarily for your benefit.

If you want to change that, you can. You don't need anyone's permission, though it would be helpful to recognize how you have given your permission to others who are trying hard to train your mind. Advertising is the most obvious example, of course, because it applies to everyone regardless of age, geography, demographics, education, etc. You might think that commercials and other forms of advertising have minimal effect on you because you know what they are and the purpose for which they were designed. But consider how many billions of dollars are spent each year on marketing and advertising. Its very existence must mean it works. Business owners aren't normally fond of throwing their money away, so you can be sure that if advertising didn't work how they want it to, they would redirect the money to something else that did or just pocket it.

The first step in taking over the training of your mind is simply to recognize and accept the fact that your mind can be trained and is being trained all the time. No matter where you are or what you're doing, your mind is active, receiving and filtering stimuli from everything around you whether you're paying conscious attention to it or not. Your brain is like the most sophisticated electrical circuit imaginable and it's constantly filtering everything in your awareness as well as things you have no conscious awareness of. Every single time you pay attention to something, you're training your mind. Even when you do it mindlessly.

The second step, like the first, is fairly simple. You <u>decide</u> to train your own mind. We may not have mental gyms to join, but just like physical exercise, we can choose to exercise the mind. Exercise is about challenge and practice, and it can be fun like Sudoku or crossword puzzles or game shows like Jeopardy! Generally, though, no one does anything consistently without first making a decision and commitment.

The third step is selection. What do you want to train your mind to do? Some options might include: improve memory, boost creativity, recognize opportunity, quiet the internal chatter, identify targets of gratitude, or see only the best in yourself and others. The possibilities are endless and it's entirely up to you as an individual to choose what's important to you. You can start anywhere and change your mind at any time. This isn't school! The only limit is your imagination and belief in yourself. That's an important limit to consider, because choosing appropriately will set you up for success while choosing unrealistically (which means something you don't actually believe to be possible for you) will set you up for failure. Remember that you have to believe it for it to be possible. Henry Ford perhaps said it best: "Whether you think you can, or you think you can't – you're right."

The final step will likely require the most effort: practice consistently and with conscious intention to improve. I did say it was exercise…

It matters how to practice. This is not the mindless repetition of the factory or school so don't approach it that way. Effective practice requires stretching past the comfort zone and into the challenge zone. It means pushing past what you thought your limits were to extend them, little by little. Be willing to accept and even appreciate the discomfort and uncertainty that go with it.

Conscious intention to improve includes two aspects that are essential to consider. The first is that improvement is all but impossible without a reliable and ideally immediate feedback loop. You need a way to evaluate whether what you're doing is working. With physical exercise you can look to muscle mass or weight changes as indicators, and you need to identify similarly measurable indicators for results of mental exercise, too. How will you know if your effort is paying off in outcomes the way you want it to? You may need to get creative on this but it can also be helped by the second aspect to consider.

Working with a trainer, though not essential, is incredibly beneficial. How do you find a mental coach? The ideal solution, of course, is to identify someone who is skilled at both what you want to get good at and at supporting others while also holding them accountable. If you already know someone like that then you just need to request their help but more likely you'll need to do some research to find the right person. Seek and you will find. You can search the Internet, tell everyone you know what you're looking for, check at local colleges and universities, consider self-help groups or meetups, or even form your own group in your community to attract like-minded others to share experiences, support, and learn from one another. Again, seek with an open mind and be creative. This is your life we're talking about, so don't just give up because you don't have all the answers at the moment. Believe that you will find what you need and look for it!

Remember that training is a process that requires patience and dedication. Growth is rarely linear so you need to be resilient and forgiving of yourself when you get off track. Just get back on again when that happens. Set achievable milestones along the way and celebrate successes. Every step in your desired direction builds momentum and you only need to see as far as the next step to keep going. Try not to worry about the future or the end of the path because that can paralyze you in place. Most of all trust yourself. Believe in yourself and the benefits of your journey for yourself and those you love so you stay motivated. Rest when you need to and don't believe anyone who says you can't succeed. It's not their mind you're trying to train!

Again, the four steps:

1. Believe you can
2. Decide to do it
3. Choose your goal
4. Practice with intention

♥

BRING IT

The one time I was struck by a spiritual bolt from the blue, I was given a deep truth that was apparently spontaneous and not in answer to any specific direct question. It was so unexpected and intense that I was unable to continue what I was doing because I felt my whole world shattering open with love and light.

The context was mundane. I was working in my home office on the accounting for my husband's business and our household. This is a task I've done for years and hated. I'm trained in business and good with numbers but I'm no accountant and get no enjoyment from tracking finances. Most of it is busy work involving data entry, syncing software with bank and credit card digital statements, assigning transactions to categories, and other such routine tasks that I find boring and time-consuming. I typically dread doing it, often putting it off until I have a stack of papers on my desk that can no longer be ignored. This just makes it worse because the more it builds up, the less I want to deal with it.

One afternoon I approached my desk with resignation to spend some time getting caught up. The sun was shining through the window and I had a feeling of loathing – on such a beautiful day working on updating the books was the last thing I wanted to do. I had been feeling really good and happy up to that point and could feel my mood sinking dramatically as I approached the computer. "God, I really don't want to be here doing this!" was the dominant thought and feeling I had.

And then the quality of the light seemed to change and this thought entered my head: this doesn't have to be drudgery – that's what you're bringing to it but you could bring your good mood to any experience if you wanted.

It's difficult to convey the effect that insight had in that moment. It was as if everything around me was infused with joy and light, demonstrating with utter conviction that I could be overwhelmed completely with peace, joy, and happiness while doing anything. What matters, I was shown, is not what you are doing but what you are bringing to it. During the experience all I could think was, this must be what enlightenment feels like.

The implications of the insight are significant. Two in particular stand out for me. The first is that I can choose to have my mood define a situation rather than allow a situation to define my mood. Subtle shift, seismic impact. If two things are connected, I can select the order of influence, especially when one of those things is an aspect of my state of being.

The second is that no matter what kind of situation I find myself in, I can bring to it whatever I may perceive as lacking in it. If accounting isn't fun for me, I can bring that quality to it by how I choose to approach it. That can mean simple things like turning on music I like or a more fundamental change in attitude like reminding myself that this work only exists and is needed because we have a business and money to manage in the first place. I choose to do it myself rather than hiring someone else to do it because it's a useful way to monitor how things are going and appreciate every invoice because it reflects work that our customers value. When I look at it this way, instead of as grunt work, I do it with a lot less resistance and more gratitude. If I can shift my thinking about this, I can do the same about anything else, too. There is always another way to look at things and I always have the option of bringing to it whatever filter I prefer. I'll be looking through one anyway so I'm better off choosing it with care.

♥

ESCAPING THE FUNHOUSE

Have you ever been in one of those carnival funhouses where there's a hall of mirrors that distorts your perception of yourself and those around you? It can be disconcerting but also fun and amusing when you're aware that what your eyes are showing you is just a trick and not reality. Without that awareness, however, it could be a frightening and disturbing experience.

The mind can seem a lot like a funhouse sometimes. One part in particular, the ego, acts a lot like a curved mirror by reflecting back a distorted and twisted version of reality that it believes to be real. It also believes so strongly in the reality of its own distortions that it can convince you thoroughly of the truth of its version and lead you down the rabbit-hole of an intense emotional ride. It can feel so real it leaves you dizzy and sick. Yesterday was like that for me.

A couple of days ago my husband did something

that I found quite upsetting. Considering how much I've been thinking and writing lately about the importance of controlling thoughts as a way of escaping emotions incompatible with peace, I chose to brush it off and not dwell on it. And that worked – at first. The next day before bed, however, something triggered my memory of it and as I lay in bed trying to fall asleep, that wave rushed back in with a force. It might have been because my guard was down when the trigger went off, or maybe I was just tired from the day but in any case, I got swept away in the negative thinking pretty quickly. He was being unreasonable and ridiculous even – my thinking went – and his actions were unfair, and how dare he treat me like a child, and so on. An added layer of irritation came from my recognition that these thoughts are preventing my sleep and I wish they'd shut up but I can't seem to stop riding this wave. This continued for maybe two hours but it felt like forever and it was exhausting. Finally my focus on quieting my mind found its mark and I fell asleep.

Less than thirty seconds after I awoke in the morning, the hateful inner dialogue was back. Throughout the day it swung back and forth between anger and sadness, and ego was firmly in control. It made a very convincing argument insisting that my husband deserved the loss of my respect for what he'd done because the action could only have been motivated by childish insecurity or simple meanness.

I tried everything I could think of to get out of the funk – meditating, listening to music, walking in nature, watching TV, even taking a long nap – all to no avail. I was sullen and withdrawn, feeling sorry for myself, frustrated, and sad. When asked what was wrong, I refused to talk about it. In that, at least, my better self prevailed.

It was as if there were two of me, or more. On one level, I felt angry, insulted, and indignant while also feeling completely justified in all of that. Yet another part of me felt trapped because it wanted to see things differently but had no idea how to. This wasn't a case where someone's actions made me feel bad about myself, which I've learned how to deal with pretty well by now, but rather it made me feel bad about the person doing the action. I couldn't find an interpretation that would make it OK for me.

After a late dinner, feeling exhausted from the emotional turbulence of the day, I got ready for bed then stepped outside for some fresh air in hopes that it would help me sleep better this night. I was still searching because I knew there had to be something I was missing; there just had to be another way of looking at things that would be more peaceful.

Looking up at the night sky, I suddenly realized something I had never really noticed before. I recognized that the behavior I objected to so strongly was entirely consistent with what I expected from this person and how I often think of him. Even if I don't dwell on the past, I still continued to look at him through the filter of every negative experience I've ever had with him. Even if the good things were enough to keep us together, they didn't erase the grievances from the past. And even if I didn't think I was holding anything against him, I had never really let go of the wrongs I felt I'd endured over the years.

This was a real revelation for me, although it shouldn't have been. It was a blind spot I didn't even realize I had. Compared to this, the thing that had been bothering me so intensely for the past 24 hours just fell away. Now that I could see the log in my own eye, the speck of sawdust in his was secondary. How could I have lived all these years with somebody I saw more often in an unflattering light than not? How is it that I have excluded the one person I'm married to from my commitment to seeing only the best in others?!

As horrific a shock as this was, paradoxically it restored my peace of mind. I suppose that could be because it put the problem squarely back in my domain, which is where I know I can solve it. I went to bed feeling grateful for the insight and with a commitment to release all past grievances so that I could drop my lens of negativity to shatter on the floor. I drifted off to sleep with this image in mind.

Waking in the morning, I felt refreshed and back on track. Interestingly enough, when my higher self makes a decision, my ego complies. Those efforts at training it are paying off! Yesterday it ran wildly off-leash and today it's back at heel with hardly a whimper. Perhaps it needs to be allowed to run at times so it can wear itself out and then submit to its master.

There are times when the ego is quite easy to subdue and others when it feels like nothing can tame it. As much as I dislike allowing it free rein, sometimes letting it go for a while is better than fighting it. As in my example from yesterday, the points it makes can be valid and its demands to be heard are often insistent. Yet it only ever sees a part of the picture, from a specific and limited point of view. In other words, I find it works much better to accept the arguments of the ego without arguing back to make it wrong, while keeping in mind that there's always more to the story that is <u>not</u> being told by the ego. If I accept it's right as far as it goes, I can still dig deeper and seek out the not-so-obvious truths buried beneath the surface of any situation. Ego can be heard, and then overruled.

This is what I mean by escaping the funhouse. If you believe the distortions of the mirrors, it can be terrifying in there. If you keep in mind the purpose for which it's designed, you can make it out unhurt and even have some fun along the way. The purpose of the ego is to keep us safe, and it reinforces in each of us a sense of individuality. But, contrary to what it thinks, it's not all there is to us. And, like a loyal dog, it needs to be put in its place because as soon as it gets the upper hand, the master loses control and just gets dragged through the mud.

AIM FOR THE TARGET

As animals, we go through life as a series of experiences that we perceive, sense, and feel in the moment. As human beings, our minds establish links between experiences and create sharable narratives in the form of stories. We tell stories all the time in so many different ways: books, movies, radio, music, podcasts, and around the campfire or kitchen table. We are all telling our stories to one another all the time. Isn't that all we talk about?

So the stories matter. This is why the minds that create the stories are such important and powerful tools. Stories shape and define our lives. But shouldn't it be the other way around?

In what might seem an odd analogy, our minds can be considered like rifles. To work properly, they need to be cared for appropriately. And when you're shooting, you don't keep your eyes focused on the gun itself, you focus on the bulls-eye. When our minds are preoccupied with the troubles all around, they're not focusing on the target.

Training the mind is about learning to focus on the target, not distractions or even obstacles. Control your mind and focus it on what you want.

♥

WAIT... WHAT'S LOVE GOT TO DO WITH MIND CONTROL?

You may wonder why a book with a title about love has so much to say about controlling your thoughts and focusing your mind on desired outcomes. The reason is simple, though perhaps counter-intuitive: learning to control your own mind is a foundational act of love.

In his book, *Stillness Speaks*, Eckhart Tolle says, "Feeling the oneness of yourself with all things is love." Put another way, love is what we call it when we feel a deep emotional connection to something or someone. This necessarily reflects a positive association between ourselves and the object of our love. Is it possible to connect through love with something or someone your mind refuses to accept and thinks badly of? Is it possible to love your life or approach living it with a loving attitude when your thoughts about it are a jumbled mass of confusion or negativity?

Getting control of your mind is what allows you to

clear a space for love to enter your awareness and grow. All forms of negative thinking are weeds that choke out the seedlings of your desires by stealing the focus of your mental energy and redirecting it away from what you want toward what you don't. This means that failing to control and focus your mind doesn't only take your eyes off your target, interfering with your ability to achieve your goals in life. It also starves love (which is your connection to what gives you joy and peace) to feed ego (which is your separate sense of self). An uncontrolled mind is most often dominated by ego, and since ego is the source not of love but of separation it is impossible for an ego-centered mind to create love, nurture it, appreciate it, or extend it. Yet what you most desire to experience in your life, whatever that is, is reachable only by the bridge of love you extend to it. Ego knows only how to build walls, not bridges.

This is why training your mind is a foundational act of love. Loving something establishes a connection between it and you. You can feel that connection when you focus on it and it fades when your attention goes elsewhere. As you gain control over your mind so you can focus its attention on what you love instead of the thousands of distractions pulling in every other direction, your connection to what you love is strengthened. As it grows stronger, you experience greater satisfaction and pleasure from it. The untrained mind, on the other hand, is preoccupied with obstacles and problems that disrupt the connection, leading to feelings of frustration.

As you train your mind, you also learn to discern

subtle distinctions, and these are sometimes crucial. For example, I love the Tesla Model X and I want one. I think about it in terms of, "When I get my Tesla…" or "My next car will be a Tesla." I have the colors and options all picked out already. My daughter and I play a game where whoever first spots a Tesla on the road "zaps" the other to acknowledge it. This is all a fun game that reminds me of my feeling of connection through my love of that car. It's exciting to imagine myself behind the wheel of exactly the one I like best. This is an aspect of how I train my mind to focus and even just notice what I like and desire.

Here is where the subtle distinction comes in. Another way I could focus on a Tesla that would be counter-productive would be if I paid attention every time I opened the door of my Prius and focused on the fact that it's not a Tesla. I could look at what I have and see it as deficient because it's clearly <u>not</u> the thing I wish I had. I might still be thinking of a Tesla, but the actual focus of my thoughts in that case would be on the disappointment or dissatisfaction at the lack of it. That would cut my happy connection to the thought of what I like and replace it with an unhappy connection to the thought of not having what I like.

The whole point of training my mind in the first place is to improve both my life and my experience of it. I care a lot about these kinds of subtle distinctions because they can be the difference between happiness and misery. I may not need a Tesla to be happy, but I definitely don't need my thoughts of wanting one to make me miserable. "I like Teslas and would love to have one" is a thought establishing my connection to a desirable future that I'm motivated to work toward making my present reality match up to, and this makes it worthy of allowing my mind to dwell on. "How can I make it happen?" is the thought that naturally follows. These kinds of thoughts keep me focused on my desire and lead me toward it. "There's no way I could afford it" or "No car is worth that much", etc., cuts me off from a dream and calls it impossible, so this thought is unworthy of more than a passing glance. Even if I may be unable to completely exclude such thoughts from my mind, I don't have to give them the prime space in the center of my attention. They might glide around in the background and even try to steal center stage, but they will soon fade away without the energy from the limelight of attention. The limelight is reserved for the stars of the show: what gives meaning, joy, love, happiness, and peace to my life.

Choosing these thoughts over negativity like complaints and criticisms is a demonstration of love for self and others. It's an affirmation of your connection to what you want for your life. As you focus on your love in this way, it becomes more central in your experience and this has a positive ripple effect outward. You feel better and happier as your disciplined thoughts hold you up rather than dragging you down. From there your positive mood spreads to the people around you and helps to boost them upwards as well. Your growing strength and skill at mastering your own mind also makes you far less susceptible to the often negative effects of other people's thinking. Protecting yourself from that is a whole other subject and it isn't trivial, but first you must learn to protect yourself from the negativity inside your own head. Focus on love, and all else falls away.

FOLLOW THE PATH OF LEAST RESISTANCE

"Resistance is futile." "What you resist persists." Perhaps these ideas are part of why Mother Teresa said, "I was once asked why I don't participate in anti-war demonstrations. I said that I will never do that, but as soon as you have a pro-peace rally, I'll be there."

This subtle distinction may seem absurd at first glance. Shouldn't anyone who is "pro-peace" also automatically be "anti-war"? Isn't it just word games to say otherwise?

There are several reasons why it's not. First, consider that "anti-war" calls to mind an image of war, not peace. The absence of war is also not the same as the presence of peace. Our whole history of "Cold War" with the Soviet Union demonstrates this clearly. Even now, as US-Russian relations are increasingly strained, our two countries are not at war but the relationship could hardly be called peaceful.

We have a long history of declaring "war" on things we resist: war on poverty, war on crime, war on cancer, war on drugs, and war on terror are the most obvious. Not one of these "wars" has ended in victory – and, in fact, many people acknowledge that just the opposite has occurred, as the problems have gotten <u>worse</u>.

This is why resistance is not just futile, it's dangerous. That's partly because thinking in terms of "anti" anything fixes that "anything" more firmly in our minds. "Don't think of a pink elephant" doesn't work because the mind cannot easily identify the "not" part so it takes the easy route of picturing the thing it <u>did</u> hear.

Taking a step back, we can see the danger of resistance on another level. What is resistance, but holding ourselves in opposition to something? As an act of separation, resistance is the fruit of the ego and therefore inconsistent with love. It is incapable of producing peace or happiness.

Physics teaches us that for everything there is an equal and opposite reaction. The implication of this is that the more force is exerted in one direction, the stronger the force in the opposite direction becomes. Whatever you choose to fight, you are establishing its existence more firmly in your experience. When you swim in a river, you feel the force of the current most powerfully when you swim upstream. So it is with the energy of emotion.

If you feel yourself being dragged into a current of spiraling negativity, following the path of least resistance would seem to pull you deeper into it. Remember that you have more than two choices –

fighting to swim upstream or giving in to swim downstream. Releasing resistance is not about choosing to move actively downstream. Rather, it's about conserving energy so you can look around for something to grab onto and stay in place or find a destination to swim toward sideways so that you're working with the momentum of the current instead of against it to get out of it.

You might think that staying in place is an undesirable option but sometimes it's the best one temporarily. It's better than continuing on toward a waterfall, for example. It gives you a little space to rest from the struggle and re-assess your situation. Sometimes you have to be still to see a way out that you may not have noticed before.

If you can recognize resistance as a trap the ego sets to get you back in the whirlpool, that awareness opens a new possibility to respond differently. For example, I shared a little bit about a recent conflict I had with my husband and my attempts to resolve it peacefully at least in my own mind. As I've said earlier about other things, it's not a matter of making a one-time decision that magically removes the problem for good. It's a decision that has to be made and repeated again and again, not just on a daily basis but sometimes every hour or even more often. When you decide to go in a new direction, that course change most often brings resistance. If you're starting to go away from the momentum of familiar patterns and ingrained habits, the resistance to change can be substantial. So although I've had a lot of practice controlling my thinking in other situations, I've still encountered a lot of resistance from my ego on this one. Not only that, it even knows when the best time of attack is, so it brings up its grievances when I'm going to sleep at night or immediately as I start to wake in the morning. It launches sneak attacks when my mind is most unguarded and vulnerable. And it succeeds a lot more often than I'd like.

What I find works best for me when that happens is to start with just noticing and acknowledging to myself that I've gotten caught up in upsetting thoughts and emotions. I watch out for self-condemnation and if I start to put myself down for any aspect of the situation or my response to it, I say to myself, "This is hard, I'm doing my best, and there has to be another way." If those feelings are directed at someone else, I tell myself something like, "OK, that may be, and what kind of person do I want to be in response?" When that doesn't work, such as when I'm too caught up in the emotion to step outside of it even for a moment, I've found it helpful to try another tack. Yesterday morning exactly that happened.

I was feeling indignant (again) that something I like and value was taken away from me and I was especially angry because it felt petty, condescending, and unfair. My ego has been actively proposing counter-attacks, mostly along the lines of refusing to do things for him that I don't enjoy doing because he took something from me just because he doesn't like it. Tit for tat. If I give and you refuse to, then I can say no, too! These are the thoughts that had overtaken my mind persistently. Trying to resist them or even quiet them seemed only to increase their intensity.

At one point the thought crossed my mind that I could make a powerful point and probably get back the thing that he took from me by doing something that doesn't hurt him directly – because doing that would backfire in two ways. A direct tit for tat response would provoke him to just dig in his heels more firmly, and it would make me exactly as the thing I was condemning (i.e., petty and selfish in choosing an action specifically to hurt someone else). So my ego's ingenious plan was to strike out at him indirectly by hurting myself.

The idea was to buy a couple bottles of wine and pour a big fat glass right in front of him. He has really been happy that I haven't been drinking so he would certainly say something. I already knew exactly what I'd say. I'd offer a toast to the thing he took and point out that wine is a worthy substitute. It has the advantage of helping me sleep better (from drinking enough to pass out – along with a subtle barb that "it's your fault I'm not sleeping well" that doesn't have to be said directly). And, if you drink enough, you can forget your troubles and bad feelings.

So the tack I took was to imagine this scenario, and it was satisfying. I decided that I would follow up and do it that evening. This satisfied the ego and it calmed down because it had a plan. I did not follow through and actually do it, however.

By agreeing in the moment that I would do it later, I bought myself some space and time. Later is crucial, because if I had acted immediately to go out and buy the wine, setting in motion the fulfillment of the plan, this tack would have backfired, too. It would have pushed me into doing something impulsively that I know I would have later regretted. By delaying acting on that ego-based decision, I gave myself room to reconsider after the emotional intensity receded somewhat. I could make a better decision, one that aligns with who I want to be, when I was no longer under emotional duress in the heat of the moment.

Following the path of least resistance means avoiding the urge to frame things as binary, "either-or" choices and in particular avoiding taking a position in opposition to anything. Whatever you feel opposed to, instead of fighting it try to use it to define what specifically you are <u>for</u>. Just as the Japanese martial art of Aikido aims to redirect the momentum of an attack rather than resisting it by countering or blocking, you can apply the same principle to mental attacks. Affirm your commitment to what you are in favor of. Give your energy to <u>that</u>.

When we consider something trivial or unworthy of attention we sometimes say, "Pay it no mind." Why do we use the language of money ("pay") in the context of our minds and attention? Perhaps it comes from an understanding that how we use our minds and attention is a very real form of investment in our future. "Pay" implies exchange, the giving of something in return for something else of equivalent value. Paying attention means to give your focused awareness so it might be useful to consider what you get for your payment. Who you pay determines what you get. Resistance is <u>always</u> a payment for exactly what you don't want! Pay, instead, for what you prefer by giving your attention to <u>that</u>. Any time you feel resistance, you can see it as a flag drawing your awareness to the fact that your attention is misdirected. Approach it with curiosity – what is the resistance telling you about what you <u>do</u> want? Figure that out and redirect your mind and attention there. Again. Again. Again...

♥

LOOK FOR THE GIFT

In every situation there is a gift. Sometimes we can find it quickly and usually it's rather obvious in circumstances we call "good." These gifts can be superficial pleasures, unexpected delights, and even substantial benefits we may have long pursued. The challenge, of course, arises when the situation at hand is challenging, painful, or worse. Yet it is often precisely these most difficult experiences that bring us the most profound and potent gifts.

No one would choose consciously to undergo a horrifically painful experience, of course. Yet people all too frequently suffer from painful or life-threatening diseases, loss of health or income from accidents or economic downturns, and even death of loved ones due to violence and all manner of other awful experiences we can imagine all too well. To be clear, nothing said here is intended to gloss over the very real pain that usually characterizes these kinds of events.

Sadly, though, bad things happen and no one is excluded from life's harsher aspects. Who can say why bad luck seems to follow some people around while leaving others alone? And often tragedies can feel very personal, so it's not really surprising that "why me?" is such a common reaction when something bad happens. The underlying assumption seems to be that "bad" people deserve "bad" things and "good" people deserve "good" things to happen to them, so when that principle seems to have been violated we get uneasy.

This idea about who deserves what and why is hugely important to us and impacts almost every aspect of our lives. It's hard to imagine any area where we don't apply it, starting most obviously with religion (heaven/hell, karma, etc.) but infusing everything else from politics and economics to education and art. All forms of reward and punishment are based on this idea that everything and everyone can be classified as "good" or "bad" (and we really dislike the ambiguity of "both").

Life seldom operates according to these neat and clear distinctions, of course. Almost everything is both at once. All it depends on is perspective. Consider the lion hunting a gazelle. If she catches it, that's a good thing (a meal) for the lion and a bad thing (death) for the gazelle. This principle applies across the board and is the reason why we sometimes hear stories about people saying, for example, that getting cancer was "the best thing that ever happened" to them. Anyone with a little life experience knows that good can come from bad and, conversely, sometimes when you win, you lose.

We can go through our lives labeling everything, judging to punish or reward. Take a look around and see the kind of world that creates.

It could be different. Many might say that dropping our judgments would create chaos and be very unfair (to the "good" ones among us, presumably). Without a system of reward and punishment, everyone would be maximally selfish, lazy, evil even. Most people who think this way clearly have a very low opinion of humanity, and surely there are good reasons for this. The difficulty is that it's kind of a "chicken-and-egg" problem because most of us tend to live up (or down) to expectations of us. Unfortunately, we've built our whole world around this "expect the worst" mentality. This creates a self-fulfilling prophecy that ensures we get precisely what we prefer to avoid.

What might happen if we flipped that on its head and chose to look for and expect the best? This is not to advocate for a naïve "stick your head in the sand" approach but rather to look at life more honestly and realistically, recognizing the truth that there is light and darkness ("good" and "bad") in everything. Who says you have to deny the difficulty to seek the gift?

When we actively look for the gift, it's like an Easter egg hunt. You don't get caught up in the empty spaces or what's not there; you keep searching until you find the treasure. You don't deny the difficulty of the hunt and you may not immediately find every last hidden treat, but you don't leave empty-handed either. And usually, the more persistently you search, the more you find.

Next time you find yourself tempted to label

something as "bad" and dismiss it, look first to see what gifts you can find. What opportunities are presented to you? Maybe it's an idea for a new business or product, a chance to make a new connection or learn something useful, or perhaps simply an occasion to show by your choices what kind of person you are in that moment. It could be a chance to practice forgiveness, patience, acceptance, or love. What gift do you see?

♥

FOCUSING ON THE POSITIVE SOUNDS LIKE SPIN… IT'S NOT

We all know what "spin" is, even if we don't think in those terms. "Put a positive spin on it" sounds like something a marketing executive might say when confronted with a problem or shortcoming in a new product. Politicians use spin all the time, such as when legislators name a law (like No Child Left Behind, which ushered in an expanded focus on standardized testing in schools as if that would solve all our problems in education). "Spin" is "a form of propaganda, achieved through providing a biased interpretation," according to Wikipedia.

When you hear the phrase "positive thinking," you may immediately think, "spin" because it often seems to be used in a way that feels deceptive. Like putting lipstick on a pig, dressing something up doesn't change what it is underneath. If you're struggling with something, whether anxiety or feelings of inadequacy at work, in your personal finances or your relationships, just telling yourself "it's OK" changes nothing and feels like a lie. So doesn't "controlling your thoughts" just mean lying to yourself?

When I speak of controlling your thoughts, I'm referring to a process of selective choosing that is based on two particular attributes that are inconsistent with self-deception. The first of these is authenticity and the other is alignment. Since alignment is a bit more straightforward, let's start there.

If you pay any attention at all to the stream of thoughts that cross your awareness, you may notice that they run the gamut from trivial to profound, uplifting to depressing and everything in between. They can seem to come from nowhere or appear to arise in clear response to something your physical senses perceive. Some of them spark excitement, like when you get an idea for how to solve a problem that has been weighing on your mind, or perhaps something reminds you of a long-held dream you have yet to realize. Others induce fear and seem to point out all the reasons why you can't count on achieving your dream. Perhaps some thoughts are more prevalent or persistent than others, but very likely they're a hodgepodge of everything.

Selectively choosing which thoughts to bestow your attention upon is an exercise in alignment. You have your car's tires aligned so the vehicle doesn't wobble down the road and shake your teeth out at high speeds, wearing the tires unevenly and possibly even compromising the safety of your car (and passengers!). Choosing thoughts from your stream of consciousness that align with your intentions for your life keeps your mental and emotional state from bouncing around so much, too. This doesn't mean there won't be curves in the road or mountainous ups and downs along the route. Nor does it mean you have to be joyfully bouncing off the walls all the time! It just means releasing the litany of self-sabotaging fear-based arguments against yourself, your dreams and your intentions for a better life however you define that. Simply put, you choose to give your attention to the thoughts that serve your purpose instead of those that undermine it.

The key difference between this and "spin" is authenticity. Authenticity means what is true for you. This is not about trying to convince yourself of something you don't believe to be true but rather about choosing to be gentle with yourself, reducing the sense of struggle. If you're dealing with something painful, such as grief or illness or loneliness, it might be completely inauthentic and even ridiculous for you to try to convince yourself that everything is fine. Yet this doesn't mean you have to dwell on whatever is causing you pain. The challenge is to acknowledge something and yet not make it central to your experience. For me, I've found the fastest way out of painful feelings is to face them, admit them, <u>feel</u> them, and then I can release them. Maybe that means curling up in the fetal position and crying, or listening to sad music, or anything else that matches my mood in the moment. In this kind of situation, controlling my thoughts might just mean reminding myself when I can that "this, too, shall pass" and I am more than this momentary feeling. It might mean only that I try to notice when I'm beating myself up over something so I can stop it. And if stopping it seems like more than I can do, I might just ask, "why do I do this?" Sometimes, though, the emotions are simply a storm that has to run its course.

While the storm is raging, I retreat into myself as much as possible. This helps to avoid provoking others to join it somehow. Some people spew all over everyone around them and this may be a release for them but serves only to spread the pain to others (many of whom, by the way, will end up spewing it right back outward again in retaliation toward the source or repetition to the next vulnerable bystander, and the cycle continues and intensifies). Isolating myself is like battening down the hatches until the fury fades. In the midst of an emotional storm, it is either too late or too early to worry much about controlling your thoughts except in one respect: try to be as gentle with yourself as you possibly can. No matter what you think about why you don't deserve gentle compassion, reach for it anyway.

Once the intensity subsides, controlling your thoughts again means acknowledging, as gently as possible, the truth of your feelings in the moment (which probably includes some relief at this point) and making a conscious effort to release all judgments you may be feeling toward yourself. You are human and that means you have feelings and they can be intense! It doesn't mean you need to judge yourself – especially if you tend to judge yourself harshly – for that. Controlling your thoughts at this stage can include reminding yourself that emotions are part of the human experience. Treat yourself as gently as you can. If you catch yourself starting to bully and beat yourself up, imagine a loving referee stepping in to stop it.

Authenticity in controlling your thoughts is about choosing the gentlest of options that feel true to you. Choose to be as kind to yourself as you possibly can. Perhaps you think you don't deserve it, or you've been taught to equate kindness and gentleness with weakness. Yet if you try it, you'll very likely see very quickly that it takes great strength to extend gentle kindness to others and perhaps especially to yourself. If you fear you lack the strength to be kind and gentle with yourself, consider how you'd treat a baby, a kitten, a puppy, or any other small defenseless creature you adore. Feel how loving and protective you are toward such a little one, how innocent and beautiful it is to you. Would you be pleased to see someone acting harshly toward this sweet little thing? Not likely.

Yet in someone else's eyes, you are every bit as precious and loved! You are just as deserving of loving, gentle kindness. When you beat yourself up, you hurt not just yourself but also everyone who loves you, and everyone you love. Devaluing yourself denies the validity of the love you give and receive. Seeing yourself as unworthy insults those who love you, and implies that those you love are only worthy of that lesser love. Loving kindness toward yourself also extends outward. Is that not a better choice?

♥

BREAKING THE CYCLE OF COMPLAINING

Perhaps the one national pastime that virtually every last one of us participates in is complaining. Some are mere amateurs while others seem to have achieved a level of professional perfection. It's hard to pinpoint exactly why it is that we use our complaints as a means for connecting with one another but I remember an incident from my childhood that might reveal a piece of the puzzle.

In fifth grade my teacher, Mr. James, would give all of us a list of words each week that we were to learn. For each word we began by writing it with correct spelling on a separate piece of paper along with its definition and a sentence using it correctly. Each Friday there was a spelling quiz. Mr. James had identified a number of students who always got 100% on the quizzes and created a separate group, and I became a part of this group. Rather than use the given list, this teacher would choose 10 or 20 words each week out of the dictionary. This was the "Hard Spelling Group" and we were challenged to learn words that far from all adults would even know. I loved language and I loved learning these words.

Once we had a cumulative test (maybe "cumulative" was one of the words we learned!). Since it covered all the words we'd learned so far, this test was a big deal and source of stress to our group. The group had maybe eight students or so, and it was split with slightly fewer girls than boys. Normally after a test or quiz we would all share our results with one another.

After Mr. James returned to us our graded cumulative tests, some of the boys in the group began sharing excitedly how well they'd done, comparing to see who'd gotten the best score. I don't remember the exact numbers but my score was higher than the ones they were congratulating themselves for and I kept it to myself at first. However, the boy who had done best among them all turned and asked me how I had done. I showed my paper and shared my excitement at how well I'd done and the boys congratulated me.

Over the next couple days I noticed that one of my friends, a girl in that same Hard Spelling Group, seemed to be avoiding me and wouldn't talk to me or play jump rope with me at recess. I was confused and asked her what was wrong. Had I done something to upset her without realizing it? I was shocked by what she told me.

She said she thought it was inappropriate that I was boasting about my spelling test score. I tried to protest that I wasn't bragging, I was just happy about the result and only shared it when I was asked directly how I'd done. If anything, the boys were bragging and she was still friendly with them and I had downplayed my success yet she held it against me.

That was a powerful lesson for me! It specifically highlighted two things. One is that what constitutes unacceptable "bragging" is very different for girls than boys, especially where other girls are concerned. The second is that it's perfectly acceptable to share with others your disappointment but can be socially risky to share your exhilaration about an achievement. Complaints are more readily accepted than celebration!

It's unclear to me why this should be the case but subsequently I began to notice that the incident wasn't an anomaly and the principle tends to apply pretty broadly. Somehow we manage to consider the success of others to reflect a weakness in ourselves. If not everyone welcomes sharing our triumphs, then little remains safe to share except our complaints.

And share them we do! We call it "commiserating," which is a perfect word for it. We share our misery with one another, not just inviting but expecting them to join us there. Do we even stop to consider that we're bringing ourselves and others down when we do that? Sure, misery loves company, but so does joy! Why is misery more popular?

As odd as it sounds, it may be the case that many people actually enjoy their misery. Could it be a form of validation, one that feels safer than joy because at least it doesn't spark envy?

If complaining is useful as a sort of social glue, the price of it is that complaining crowds out love.

Obviously we don't love the things we complain about (even if we do love the attention we get for it). Complaining is a form of rejection, while love exists only in acceptance. Since we can't have both at once, we must choose between them.

I've sometimes found it quite difficult to choose love when some of the people around me so consistently choose to complain. If I don't want to get dragged down, how can I handle that without leaving someone I love feeling invalidated?

I tried something once that worked far better than I could have expected. I was speaking on the phone with an ex-boyfriend's mother, who tended to worry a lot. She is an extremely intelligent, accomplished woman whom I admire greatly and have always had a warm and loving relationship with, even long after her son and I parted ways.

My normal response when she would talk about her concerns for her health, her son, her country's politics or whatever else, was to do what most of us do: sympathize and commiserate. This time, however, after every complaint I responded with something affirming but unrelated to the complaint. So, for example, I expressed my admiration for her and confidence in her ability to solve whatever problem confronted her. I told her I appreciated her and how much she meant to me. This was very heartfelt and spoken with conviction.

When I finished speaking, there was silence on the other end of the line. When she spoke, her tone had changed completely, she said little other than "wow, thanks" and then we hung up.

I think she was so surprised she was speechless

(something I'd never seen in her before!). And since my response was so different from what she was used to, she had no idea how to continue the conversation. Yet there felt like a real connection was made and I, for one, felt elated afterward.

Complaining is so accepted and widespread that for many of us it's reflexive and we frequently fail to recognize it for what it is. It's more than an individual behavior; it's a social dynamic. In fact, it's so universal in our culture that we tend to notice only when someone stands out for <u>not</u> complaining! My uncle is a good example – he's turning 90 this year and has had his share of health concerns but you'd never know it from talking with him. He and my aunt lead a life so active that I, at half his age, would struggle to keep up with them!

As the example of my ex-boyfriend's mother illustrates, sometimes the fastest route to a new destination is indirect. If I had said something to her to call attention to her complaining, pointing it out or asking her to stop, the most probable response would have been defensiveness. I don't want to be called a complainer, either! But by looking beneath the surface, and addressing the underlying need, I inadvertently freed her from the desire to complain. By offering her connection, validation, and love, I stumbled upon a valuable key to breaking the cycle of complaining. Best of all, the change proved lasting!

♥

THE PERFECTION OF CREATION

How do you see yourself in the context of all creation? Perhaps you think that you are small and insignificant next to the vastness of the cosmos that extends to both smaller and larger than the human imagination can encompass. Possibly you experience yourself as a grand and wondrous being that exists at the culmination of all that exists in the universe. You might even think both these things at the same time!

The one thing that neither science nor religion can prove definitively is how consciousness arose, what provided the very first spark of life. It's an astonishing mystery, existence. More religiously inclined people might call it a miracle. However you personally understand it, life and all of creation are central to who and what we are. Stop and consider for just a moment the fact that you <u>are</u>. You are here, now, in this place, aware of these thoughts being conveyed to you from this piece of paper (or maybe a digital equivalent, which is no less amazing). However you came to be here, just notice that you <u>are</u> here. You <u>are</u> a part of existence. You <u>are</u> a part of all of creation, this majestic and mysterious universe. You <u>are</u>.

That, all by itself, is enough, because it is everything. You are part of that. The part is as the whole, so you <u>are</u> that. In this, you are perfect.

SILENCING THE SERPENT

A foundational story I heard as a young Christian child was the origin story of the Garden of Eden. I've yet to meet an American who is unfamiliar with this tale of how God created Adam from the Earth, then Eve from one of Adam's ribs, and left them to dwell in the paradise of Eden. The one restriction God placed upon the pair was not to eat the fruit of the Tree of Knowledge, lest they incur God's wrath and punishment. Eve, however, was seduced by a speaking serpent to taste the fruit that appeared so delectable to her. The sneaky serpent convinced her that God had placed the temptation yet reserved from them this fruit because it would allow the partaker to become as God. Didn't she want to know that taste for herself? Thus was Eve tricked by the snake to commit the first, original sin by acting against God's will. *Genesis* tells us that God cursed all of humanity in retribution.

Who was this serpent? The story doesn't tell us directly, but the serpent has long been a powerful symbol for humans. In some cultures it represents fertility, and even in ours it also symbolizes medicine. Snakes are also seen as guardians or protectors on one hand and are associated on the other with vengefulness.

I've come to see the Garden of Eden story as allegory – not necessarily true literally but instructive of a broader truth. The classical interpretation, of course, is as a warning against disobeying the commands of God, and it offers an explanation for our inherently sinful nature. I've heard an opposite interpretation, as well, that also made a lot of sense to me: the disobedience of Adam and Eve is what first established free will, giving rise to the entire world because presumably the first pair would never have become parents had they remained in the Garden.

The serpent whispering to Eve is an interesting image because it seems to indicate that she was beguiled by an outside force, rather than acting on an impulse originating within her. (Of course, God is also an outside force in this story, so the only choices available to Adam and Eve involved reacting to external forces.) The story thus establishes the opposing forces of good and evil, which we all must choose between. Here "good" is seen as innocence and "evil" as knowledge – knowledge of good and evil in particular. It's interesting that the story seems to warn us against consuming this fruit, which allows us to see and judge things as good or evil. It might seem that the message is that knowledge is a bad thing but I think the meaning is subtler than that.

Eating from the tree of the knowledge of good and evil gives rise to the world of duality, the physical world of night and day, hot and cold, safe and dangerous, etc. This is a perspective that invites judgment because things seen as opposites appear contradictory and thus require choice. Choosing necessarily means exclusion, yet the totality of existence includes everything. God – consciousness itself – thus becomes fragmented, and set at odds against… itself. This creates heaven and hell – union with God or separation. Duality precludes unity.

Oddly enough, we can experience life in both ways. Whether we believe in God or not, we can feel ourselves connected to all of creation, all of existence, all of life. We can also feel disconnected and separate. Ultimately the difference is a state of mind, because our minds are what interprets and gives meaning to our experience.

Meditation is a mode of the mind through which we can experience the peace of unity and connection to all because it is the practice of quieting the mind. In stillness there is peace. But what are we quieting by meditating? That internal commentator, known as the ego, or the Voice of Judgment. This, I believe, is what the serpent in the story of Eden truly represents.

Personally, I would call it the Voice of Viciousness because it's a brutal critic that is never satisfied and blathers on constantly about its endless complaints. To me, it has always been a fearsome beast because it will say anything and it knows exactly how to wound me where I'm most sensitive. This vicious serpent strikes with deadly accuracy and its message is always venomous. "You're worthless," "you never get it right," "you're a loser" and countless variations on the theme are all it ever says, unless it's talking not about me, but you. "That obnoxious jerk cut me off," "what a selfish…" and much worse are the judgments it pronounces on others, too. That Voice of Viciousness is never satisfied, always complaining, and tears down everyone in its path with its evil lies.

I've spent the better part of three decades learning how to tame and silence this awful serpent. One of the more surprising things I've learned is that this Voice has little power or energy of its own. Instead, it feeds on and then perverts and turns against me my own energy. I listened recently to a podcast from James Altucher in which he interviewed author Michael Singer, who astutely observed that there's a big difference between hearing something and listening to it. This is a helpful way to understand how the Voice of Viciousness acquires its power. When I simply hear it without responding, its effect on me is very muted and limited. When I start to listen to it, however, my attention creates an active form of participation that intensifies the Voice as I engage and even identify with it. Before I understood the difference, I didn't realize that this Voice was not, in fact, me. It was so familiar and I was so used to it that it seemed like it and I were one and the same. It really clicked for me that this was not true when I heard how Eckhart Tolle put it: who is listening, who is aware of that voice? You are that awareness, and not the Voice that you are aware of. Recognizing this created the separation of myself from the Voice of Viciousness.

Once I saw that I am not that Voice, I began to distance myself from it more and listen to it less often even as I continued to hear it. I began to think of it as background noise and found that I could actually tune it out to a surprising degree. It lost a lot of its power to command me. Most importantly, it also lost most of its power to convince me that what it says about me and others is true.

This alone had a positive effect on my life that is hard to overstate. Letting go of that identification with the Voice of Viciousness was liberating in a way as profound as dropping a hundred-pound backpack while climbing a steep rocky mountain.

When I stopped believing all the nasty things that Voice was telling me, a new question was revealed: if I'm not that Voice, who am I? What does it mean if I'm the awareness that hears it? "I don't know" is a step back into uncertainty and even mystery. I felt like I had gotten to a point of not believing anything because I could not accept that anyone outside me could tell me who I am and even the voice I was so used to hearing inside me really didn't know the answer to that question, either. So how can I know?

And then the next question: how can I know anything at all, if even just knowing who or what I am is so challenging? Does anyone really know anything, or are we all just making it up as we go along? The only thing I know for sure with 100% certainty is this: I am. I exist. That is all I can know to be true with complete confidence. It's also the only thing any of us can know beyond doubt. Yet the human mind seeks to know,

<u>needs</u> to know. We will do or give anything to know, and this is the core of why science and religion are so important to us. Yet most (by which I mean <u>all</u>) of what we "know" is actually what we think and believe to be true. Reminding ourselves of this is a great exercise in humility and honesty. It's also the source of true freedom, because it's your blank slate to create your life.

Stripping everything down to that one point of knowledge – I exist, I AM – allows me to create anything I choose. I may apply a label – I am human, a gender, a race, a nationality – but no label can encompass all that I am. I can choose to identify myself with anything, and likewise refuse to allow anyone else to identify me as anything. If that's not freedom, then what is?

Simply the fact that I am is enough. Whether God created me, or millions of years of evolution did, or nothing did and I've always existed, however or whyever I am, still: I am. Just that makes me good enough, enough to be and live and choose how to live and be. Accepting that is an act of love, toward myself and everyone else, too, because it applies universally to all that is.

This is the love that has taken over my life since I've stopped listening to that judgmental Voice of Viciousness, all the time about everything. Yes, it's still there and it sometimes still ensnares me in its evil, ugly lies, but it can no longer hold me in its grasp any longer than I allow it to. When I claim my power to be free from this internal judge and jailer, I also find myself far more impervious to the judgments of others. The opinions of others are just that: their opinions, thoughts, and beliefs but they are not me or even a reflection of me. They are released from my awareness by my own love, because I can recognize them for what they are.

I find it very sad that there is almost nothing in our culture that encourages us to honor and love ourselves as we are. If anything, we've built everything upside down, reinforcing fear and criticism in everything from our self-image and our bodies to our global systems of governance and commerce. "Not good enough" is the pervasive underlying message we spread about almost everything, and especially about ourselves. We fear even love, thinking it's possible to love too much and thus encourage selfishness and narcissism when in reality these things arise as a defense against a lack of real love. Love accepts us as we are but that doesn't mean it removes our desire to be even better! Just the opposite, actually – being loved gives us strength and desire not to disappoint. The more I love myself, the more it extends outward from me and feeds my aspirations to be a better person, to be of service to others, to be the best me I can be. Love begets kindness and forgiveness, in turn replacing criticism and violence. Only the wounded and the desperate strike out at others to hurt them. Judgment is a symptom of insecurity. Love is the cure. In the presence of love, the serpent is silent.

♥

THE NATURE OF LIFE IS GROWTH

If we strip everything down to a single point of knowledge – I AM – then what? If I look at my life as a blank canvas inviting new creation, how do I know where to go from there without the paths offered by identification (with race, gender, ethnicity, nationality, etc.)? What first principles can guide me forward? One of the first things I might do is try to understand the landscape that forms the context for my existence.

Looking outward, my first concern is whether my environment is hostile or friendly. Am I safe or am I in danger? If I'm surrounded by beings who are going about their own business so that they mostly leave me alone to pursue my own path, perhaps even offering assistance or support, then this freedom feels very safe and exciting. There are so many possibilities and I can't wait to explore them! But if the opposite is true and my environment is shared with creatures who are hungry, aggressive, and violent, then this freedom feels very perilous and my best option seems to be to hide. The Garden of Eden story would seem to say we've been banished from the safe haven and forced out into the wild, terrifyingly dangerous world dominated by predators.

This may be one reason why the first reaction you might have to the idea that we are all fully free to choose for ourselves how to live is that it sounds good in theory but it would never work in reality. If they had no fear of retribution or punishment from a higher power, wouldn't people just run amok and do all kinds of horrible things to one another? Wouldn't that just be chaos and anarchy, leaving everyone dead or maimed?

Now in the 21st Century, with the benefit of thousands of years of recorded history, we have some evidence that life can be both harsh and nurturing. There is reason to believe both that humans are good and that humans are evil. In this context, freedom is exciting and terrifying.

Aside from the underappreciated fact that we have a choice about how to think about this, for me it's helpful to recognize and remember that the nature of life is growth. To me this suggests that the future is more hopeful than the past might indicate. Since growth encompasses more than just physical properties, and we humans are capable of learning from our experiences, I find more hope than fear in freedom.

Life seems to exist in the tension between hope and fear, past and present. Fear, of course, serves an essential purpose in alerting us to danger so we can avoid it and seek safety, but it can also paralyze us, and being in a chronic state of fear is deadly. Unfortunately, our modern world manages to magnify fear even as most of us are far safer overall than our ancestors ever were. It would be bad enough if this fear only caused individuals to hide, but it has much farther-reaching consequences. It also compels us to curtail freedom for everyone.

We do this in more ways than I can count. It's important to recognize that fear is the primary enemy of freedom. At the same time, freedom is our natural state and fear is a learned response. This can be seen very clearly when we look at the generation gap. Small children are naturally fearless and curious, and they seem to lack all concept of limitation. They persist in pursuing what they want, are open to everything, and live with joyful abandon. This is something of an exaggeration, of course, but probably only to the extent that a child has already absorbed the fearful anxiety of parents or other caregivers. The point is that although it's true that individuals may differ markedly, the overall general tendency holds that the young are carefree while their elders with more life experience are much more cautious.

To be clear, I'm not advocating here that we should just throw caution to the winds and do anything we want without regard for consequences. Nor am I saying that we should turn our backs on traditions and the lessons of our individual or collective life experience. It would, however, be wise to avoid the temptation to reject the possibility that elders may have more to learn from the young than teach them. "Learning from experience" can too easily be code for closing off options, closing our minds, and holding ourselves back from pursuing our hearts' desires. "I already tried and it didn't work so it's not worth trying again" is an attitude that's all too common among adults (especially middle age and older), but you never hear a kid say that. Growth is never about staying in one place or stopping because we've already tried unsuccessfully. Growth is always about pushing into new frontiers and taking opportunities (which is just another word for "risks" but with a more positive and hopeful tone).

What could be possible if we chose to live from the perspective of just this understanding: I am alive, and the nature of life is growth. If this were all we needed to know about ourselves and one another, there would be no need to insist that anyone else believe anything in particular, although we could all choose any beliefs or attributes to identify ourselves with. We could free ourselves from the tyranny of needing other people to do or be what we want them to because we would base all our relationships on the understanding that we are all meant to be here (proven by the very fact that we are), we are all valuable and worthy exactly as we are (again, proven by the simple fact of our existence), and all free to grow and express who we are as we choose.

This would transform the world into a far better place than it is now for most people. This is true for at least two reasons. The primary one is that human culture would center around a universal message of "you're good and you matter" instead of the opposite. The second is an outgrowth of the first: love and acceptance are antithetical to pathology, so fewer damaged people means less crime and violence. More than that, we would give our respect and admiration to those who best embody the principles and show by example how to live as our best selves, so others would be reminded to strive for the same.

"You're good enough" is no recipe for laziness or selfishness because those things are incompatible with growth and would therefore be discouraged by the culture. "We are good and seeking to be better still" is an inspiring message that would allow all people to live with greater peace, joy, and love. It helps us to support and encourage one another to bring out the best in us instead of the worst. It reflects a true reverence for life.

♥

KINDNESS IS THE KEY TO THE DOORWAY TO LOVE

Have you ever had the experience of being in a foul mood, when everything seemed to be going against you, and suddenly out of the blue somebody offered you the gift of pure kindness? Maybe it was something small, like the person with a full cart of groceries ahead of you in line who waved you around to go first or the person in the car ahead of you in the drive-thru lane who paid for your coffee. Maybe it was something more significant but in any case an unexpected kindness brightened your day. If that's ever happened to you, then you know how touching the experience can be. Perhaps you've been on the giving end and you can still remember how great or even giddy you felt doing something unexpectedly generous for someone else.

Acts of kindness, whether random or not, open the hearts of both giver and receiver. They remind us of our shared humanity and make us smile with happiness. Sometimes it makes a good day even better, and other times it shines a ray of light through the storm clouds. The gift of kindness is one of the most valuable things we can offer one another, yet it doesn't have to cost us anything to give. I wonder why we don't do it more often.

We humans, as social animals, are very sensitive to the moods and emotional states of others. We match up and mimic them, often without even realizing we're doing it. We all know how one sourpuss can drag a whole room down, whether at work or a family get-together during the holidays. When someone with infectious enthusiasm enters the room at a party, you can just hear the new buzz of excitement.

When I lived in St. Petersburg, Russia, I had the privilege of working for a woman who was (and is) masterful at bringing out the best in others. She is, hands down, the best boss I ever had and one of the best friends. She would arrive to the office with a bright and cheerful "hello!" every day, regardless of the weather (which could be brutal) or cultural norms (like Americans, Russians tend to be quite serious at work, and smiles are reserved mostly for family and close friends). She was an American who spoke no Russian, so it had to have been challenging for her working there, but the only attitude she ever showed was optimistic, supportive, and friendly. She focused almost exclusively on the strengths of our team members, making everyone feel valued as experts in their field. She's the kind of person you really don't want to disappoint, and she was uncommonly generous with her praise and mentorship. She inspired intense loyalty and admiration for all of these reasons. Her authentic concern and care for others shines through everything she says and does. Even now, in her 70s, she's living in Ghana for a year, working to make life better for others.

In the 20 years since I worked for her, we've stayed friends and I've learned that her unfailing optimism and kindness are the result of her conscious choice to be that way. She makes a point to look for the best and even when she encounters disappointment, she's honest about it without being bitter or dramatic about it.

Maybe you know someone like this, too. I know that for me, she has been a tremendous inspiration and someone I'm endlessly grateful to have in my life. I've learned from knowing her that no matter what I face, I can choose to respond with kindness and I know from experience what a difference that can make for others. I've also learned what a difference it can make for me when I choose to be kind in difficult situations.

♥

YOU MATTER

Choosing to be kind to yourself and others is a powerful affirmation and demonstration of the essential fact that every human being has value. This value is completely independent from specific attributes of personality, experience, or identification with any group because it arises from the fact of your very existence. It is a universal value that reflects the worth of life itself. It is universal because it is common to all, without regard to circumstances, including physical characteristics and social or financial standing. Regardless of what else we may choose to value in people, the universal worth of life is a baseline value that is the very foundation for all that we may choose to build our lives around. We can call it human dignity, human rights, or the fundamental value of life – at its core it is our recognition that existence has meaning. Rejecting this fundamental principle would erase all basis for civilization and shared society.

Acceptance of this basic idea does, however, impart certain responsibilities on all of us. First among these is to act in accordance with the principle because otherwise it is meaningless. But what exactly does it mean to act accordingly?

The right to exist is the first principle and respect for it obviously means, at a minimum, allowing what already is, to be. Murder and otherwise killing any human being clearly violates this first principle and is therefore unacceptable. The same principle applies to animals and plants, with the notable exception being that eating requires killing in some form. This, too, is simply a fact of existence and obviously not negotiable but truly valuing life even when we take a life to eat implies responsibility for how that is done.

I think of kindness as the natural and even inevitable response that arises from the authentic acceptance of the first principle. If I truly value life and hold it in esteem, then behaving toward it in any way other than kindly is unnatural. When I value anything, I am necessarily defining it as "good" (otherwise, how can it be said that I value it?). When I consider something to be good at its most basic level, I obviously don't treat it dismissively or harshly; I treat it with gentleness, kindness, and reverence, even. Observable acts of kindness, then, are a reliable indicator of what I truly value.

This point seems basic and obvious, so much so that the discussion of it might come across to some as condescending. I offer it here because sometimes the most obvious things can be neglected but even more because turning basic truths around can sometimes most effectively reveal what is otherwise obscured, like missing the forest for the trees. In this case, I can turn around the logic of what I've just described to ask: What does our observation of the current level of kindness in our culture reveal to us about the true value we put on life?

Every unkindness is a devaluation of life in one way or another. There are so many excuses and justifications we use collectively to devalue life: sometimes it's based on behavior (e.g., criminal) but shockingly often it's based on some aspect of identity (e.g., being Black in America, Muslim, etc.). The unspoken implication is this. The value of life itself is universal, so when we devalue the lives of Black, Muslim, or any other sub-class of people we are setting a correspondingly lower level for the value of any and all life. We all know intuitively that this is true even if we don't think or talk about it in such explicit terms. If my life can be devalued, then so can yours.

My personal choice is to accept and embrace the first principle that life itself has value, in fact that it has supreme value above all else. If Life is not the supreme value, then what could possibly have any value at all?

If it has supreme value, then life is the greatest good for the reason I described earlier. And if life is good, then it necessarily follows that I am good and you are good (because we are alive). I possess all of the value of life, as do you and every other person alive. This means I must value myself accordingly, and value you the same. And this must apply universally because to devalue any life is to devalue Life.

The Black Lives Matter movement in this country

sparked some controversy when some (non-Black) people understood the statement as a comparison and assertion of the value of some lives over others. The response that "All Lives Matter!" can be seen essentially as an assertion that "we do not accept the idea that we and our lives don't matter (which our exclusion from the statement "Black Lives Matter" would seem to imply)." As far as it goes this is fair yet it misses a crucial point that Black Lives Matter activists had been drawing attention to: it is precisely Black lives that this country has historically and continues to this day to devalue, and if all lives truly matter then Black lives must also matter as much as any life does. Drawing attention to Black lives specifically is thus appropriate precisely because in this country Black lives have never been valued equally with White lives.

We must face truth and look honestly at what or who we do or do not value precisely because the value of life is universal. This is the reason why the only path to peace is to value life singularly. There can be no exceptions or qualifications to this. **This, then, is what Love is: to value Life singularly as the supreme value**.

I am alive and I matter.

You are alive and you matter.

We are alive, we matter, and we are supremely valuable.

This is Love, and it is for you. It is your birthright, to give and receive.

THIS LOVE IS FOR YOU

"The greatest risk we'll ever take is by far
To stand in the light and be seen as we are."[7]

This is the Love that gives birth to peace, kindness, forgiveness, and joy. Call it what you will, but accepting this deeply and living by it is your most basic choice as a human being and it is a choice you make alone, on your own, as the truest expression of your inherent freedom. It is a choice always available to you, regardless of any external circumstances. It is the one freedom that cannot be taken from you unless you agree willingly to give it up. Even if you have waived this fundamental right at any time in the past, you can reclaim it whenever you want simply by choosing to. Choose to value Life singularly as the supreme value and you are choosing Love for yourself and others. Choose Love and it becomes clear that Love is within you, available to you always, and in fact it becomes who you are in your experience. You are worthy of it, and it is yours for the choosing, no matter what anyone else thinks, says, or does. You choose.

---

[7] "Stand In The Light" from the album, *Something Beautiful* by Jordan Smith.

♥

ABOUT THE AUTHOR

Kimberly Carlton is a lifelong seeker and student of love and spiritual growth. She has devoted her career to educating and supporting people who are committed to controlling their own destiny. As a nonprofit executive and entrepreneurship educator, she has taught thousands of people how to improve their lives financially. A graduate of Pomona College and the Stanford Graduate School of Business, she is passionate about encouraging people to follow their dreams.

www.ingramcontent.com/pod-product-compliance
Lightning Source LLC
Chambersburg PA
CBHW072002040426
42447CB00009B/1449